Terminal Freedom

Daniel Keys Moran
Jodi Moran

Dedication

Kevin Daniel Moran, the tea-drinking, running, jumping, climbing, utterly amazing Child Athlete From Hell, whose first words were "Thank you," who cried when we wouldn't let him climb up into our laps when we were writing, and who tried to help us write when we did let him sit with us, smacking at the keyboard (occasionally improving the text); and who, in the way of children, loves us both almost as much as we love him.

Notices

"Terminal Freedom" is copyright © 1998 by Daniel Keys Moran and Jodi Moran.

The cover is copyright © 2002 by Daniel Keys Moran.

The right of Daniel Keys Moran and Jodi Moran to be identified as the authors of this work has been asserted in accordance with the Copyright, Designs and Patents Act 1988.

All rights reserved. No part of this publication may be reproduced, stored in a retrieval system, or transmitted in any form or by any means, electronic, mechanical, photocopying, recording or otherwise, without the prior permission of the publisher.

Note:

This is FSAnd Version 1.1 of this text.

If this is a pirated copy of the fsand.com edition of Daniel Keys Moran and Jodi Moran's "Terminal Freedom," you can do the right thing and support the authors of this book by going to fsand.com and buying a copy for yourself. Once you've purchased it, you can refer it to your friends and fellow readers and make ongoing referral fees from their purchases. For more information about the fsand referral program, and how it can actually help you to make money from your reading, go to fsand.com/faq.

If you've purchased this book, you are forever entitled to a new download of the book, whenever a new edition is issued for the sole purpose of correcting errors. If you've noticed errors yourself, you can come to fsand.com/text to suggest copy editing corrections, and if the author approves we'll roll them into the next edition of the book.

Introduction by eluki bes shahar

WHEN I WAS very young and calculating my age in single digits or close to it; innocent enough to believe that all adults were Automatically Cool; I was standing with my mother in the basement of one of the big department stores in Oakland with an extorted dollar clutched in my hand, staring at a rack of books. The one I chose, I chose almost at random, but to this day I remember it won out by inches over a book about James Bond's nephew. It cost me 60 cents. I took it home, and read it, and was catapulted into an amazing universe of wonder and rollick and Really Neat People, all of whom had the most interesting lives I could conceive of and were frequently witty besides. I have that book to this day, though I haven't opened it in years; I must have read it a hundred times in my troubled adolescence; it was for me Tarzan's Africa, PC Wren's Algeria, Graustark, and Oz.

The book was *The Butterfly Kid,* by Chester Anderson, and it gilded New York City with a glamor that it holds to this day for me, and caused me to develop an unremitting passion for Michael the Theodore Bear (much too dignified to be called Teddy, don'cha see?)

Okay. So it may never make anybody's top ten list, and you already think I'm a honkweasel for giving you this long screed on a book you've never heard of. But you miss the point. This book was *magic*. The story it contained had the power to transform my life, and I don't think that's too grandiose a statement.

What I want to say is this: there's only one book like that in everyone's life, and more often than not, you come to it young. But last night, reading *Terminal Freedom,* I felt a ghost of that old magic sweep over me, and I knew then that somewhere out there, waiting without knowing it, are the people for whom *Terminal Freedom* will be that sort of touchstone; a book that becomes part of what they really are.

Contents

Dedication..iv
Notices..vi
Introduction by eluki bes shahar...viii
I Love L.A..1
Terminal Sue..7
Bogie Freedom...13
Detecting..21
Ten Percent..33
Strangers In The Night..43
Land Sharks...57
People Were After Him...71
Visitors...81
Claudia...89
Pie Heaven...97
Evil From The Depths Of Hell..107
Tawdry Sex..113
Dreadful Sam...123
What The World Is Coming To..127
Answers..133
Kidnapped..147
Preparing To Rambo In Fontana...155
Ramboing In Fontana..165
A Real American Hero..175
The Complete History Of
The World Up To This Point...183
Space Nazis From Hell..189
Walkin' Talkin' Dave...195
Ramboing at the Disneyland Hotel.......................................201
Ass Over Teacup...213
The Happiest Place On Earth..223
Red Is The Rose, Red Is Redemption...................................229
Epilogue...247

TERMINAL FREEDOM

I Love L.A.

A MILLION AND one angels watch over the city. The flutter of their wings causes a breeze to shiver through the heights of the palm trees.

The City of Angels, the jewel of the Pacific Rim, a diamond burning in the Ring of Fire, the brightest and the best of all the cities in the world. It is in fact the most beautiful place on Earth. Randy Newman said it best: "Everybody's very happy, cause the sun it shines all the time."

The buildings rise up haphazardly, half-burned in riots and arson attacks, damaged in floods, mud slides, and earthquakes. Murals depicting flowers and space ships and Jesus dying on the Cross cover the cracks in the walls.

There are no murals of angels. The angels are everywhere.

On Watseka they'll offer you blessings and vegetarian food, and around the corner on Robertson they'll steal your running shoes, but you won't mind because your stomach's full, and the sidewalk's always warm in the city of Angels.

Be careful crossing the streets; the glitter of shattered glass reflects back up off the black pavement like art.

People tip refrigerators into the cement-lined Los Angeles river, and the river likes it. When you're a river and you've been completely walled in, you get your joys where you can.

The river rushes toward the ocean, pouring into the Pacific at Long Beach and mixing with the sewage that has drifted down from Santa Monica Bay. In Santa Monica at the pier there are carousel horses, spinning for eternity, and signs on the beach saying "Don't Go In The Water." And we don't go in the water, and not because we're afraid of the sharks, oh no. (And at the Biltmore Hotel in downtown Los Angeles we can order the Santa Monica Bay Chowder; only we don't do that either.)

In either direction, going south to Venice or north to Malibu, brave locals get in the water and surf. They stand on their boards, and scream at God until he knocks them over, and in the heavens, God laughs, because he knows the filth in Santa Monica Bay has filtered south past Venice, and north past Malibu. God's not the vindictive type, but he figures that if you piss in the water you surf in, that's your cancer.

Get out of the ocean on a good gang day, and the Crips and Bloods and Thirty-Second Streeters and all the other miscellaneous little gangs whose names don't make it onto television will mow you down with their black rubber-grip leave-no-fingerprints guns. The gangsters wear shorts that come down to their knees and socks that come up to their knees. They wear tank tops that let their shoulders burn and then they go home and tell people they've been to the beach. They don't mention the murders.

Police helicopters, with news choppers trailing them, beat their way across the sky, spotlights burning down into the city, searching for felons in stolen cars. In Monte Carlos and Cadillacs, Buick Regals and Crown Victorias. They steal foreign cars for the parts. They steal American cars for the cars. They lower them and lacquer them. Look down into an inch of stolen lacquer and you'll see your soul.

Of course it will be distorted by the flecks of gold, deep in the paint, but it will be your soul nonetheless.

Looks good, doesn't it?

NOT LONG AFTER sunset, in the heavens above the city, the angels shift, creating a path, allowing a shimmering needle of light to descend from the sky and into the city they watch over.

The million and first angel, Our Lady, the Queen of the Angels, watches the man arrive, and smiles.

THE NEEDLE OF light crashes in the middle of Hollywood Boulevard, and everybody looks. They all know it's a promotional gimmick, but they look anyway. It's not interesting, it's not new, but it's better than nothing. The doors open and a man steps out of the glowing structure, wearing a black jumpsuit with gold epaulets on his shoulders, and shimmering silver ribbons across his chest. He looks like a spaceman and he's holding his breath. He knows he can breath the air, but he's afraid. Christ, there are millions, billions of humans breathing it right that minute. But that was where the fear came in. How could they all be breathing the same air at the same time?

He exhales with a gasp, and sucks in the carbon-monoxide laden air, and goes into a fit of coughing. He had been told, by people who had breathed this air before, that it would be sweet. He's been lied to, which you'd think he'd be used to by now –

An RTD bus drives by him, inching its way past the obstruction in the middle of Hollywood Boulevard, belching black smoke. The driver flips the man off without really looking at him. The man doesn't notice; he's choking to death, while the needle of light behind him is getting brighter and very hot.

Zooming down the street, following the trail of black smoke emitted by the bus, are two boys on skateboards. One of them is a white boy, with long blond hair and a fierce tan, and the other is a black boy with dreadlocks that reach his butt. They reach the man, hunched over on his knees in the middle of Hollywood Boulevard. They slow, hesitating, watching the man pityingly. That had been a good bit of bus smoke he'd sucked in.

The man straightens slowly and staggers away from the glowing needle. Rivulets of molten metal drip from the needle, onto the road, and sizzle. The boys ignore the self-destructing promotional gimmick; they've seen better. They follow the staggering man and skate around him, circling him once, twice, a third time. The man spins with them, dizzily, trying to keep them both in his sight at the same time, marveling. He's never seen anything that looks like the boy with the dreadlocks – or for that matter, anything that looks much like the fearsomely tanned blond boy.

Finally, the boy with dreadlocks says, "Good looking suit."

The blond frowns. "Looks hot, though."

THE MAN LOOKS at his stolen clothing in the reflection of a storefront window. His shirt is a wild Hawaiian print, blue and red and green and yellow and orange, with a touch of gold, hanging open to expose a radiation-darkened chest. There are parrots and palm trees on his shirt, but he doesn't know the words for either of them. He knows that one's a bird, and the other's some kind of weed, and he knows he likes them. His pants are dark blue and baggy and reach barely past his knees, and his rope sandals, woven from hemp with all the life smoked out of it, are the perfect final touch.

He wiggles his toes.

The kid on the skateboard had been right – he *had* been hot.

Now he's cool.

Five Years Later....

...Five Years Later

Terminal Sue

"IT'S EIGHTY-FIVE dollars an hour. You pay a thousand twenty as a retainer before I begin work. That buys twelve hours. When the retainer is used, you pay me another retainer. You don't argue with me. Ever. You don't whine if I tell you something you don't like. I'm in charge. Not you. You pay the bills and you don't argue. Is that clear?"

Terminal Sue watched him as she spoke. He seemed to be taking it well. When she finished, she paused and waited for him to say yes.

He said, "Yes."

"Good. Give me your problem and your name and the thousand twenty, in reverse order."

From the window of her office, Terminal Sue had watched the man get out of his car. She had known, from the way the guy looked around the parking lot, shifty-eyed and nervous, that he was coming to see her. He looked like a wannabe rock and roll star: three earrings in each ear, blond-haired and blue-eyed, a thin body that owed more to cocaine than to Nautilus. He wore blue jeans, snakeskin boots, and a leather bomber jacket that might have seen service in World War II. His hair was tied back into a long pony tail by a blue bandanna. Terminal Sue smiled. Crip colors. Some Blood was going to shoot his ass and he wouldn't even know why.

She wondered where he was from. No native Angeleno would have made that particular mistake.

He had jumped when he slammed the door of his Mazda Miata, startled by the sound he'd created. Now, sitting across the desk from Terminal Sue, looking anywhere but into Terminal Sue's cold black eyes, he seemed uncertain how to begin.

She didn't especially care how he began, as long as he had the thousand and twenty dollars. She already knew what his problem was; she could see it in his weaselly eyes and his too-tight pants. A woman. Only he was going to call her a chick.

"My name is Carlo. Carlo van Zandt. And there's this chick —"

Terminal Sue smiled. "A thousand and twenty dollars. Up front. I know I said that."

"Just to hear what I have to *say*?"

"If I don't like what you say," Terminal Sue said, "I'll give some of it back."

"How much?"

"Nine hundred and thirty-five dollars. Unless you piss me off, in which case I'll charge you for another hour."

Carlo stared at her. "I don't have that much cash. Do you take checks?"

"No. Visa, MasterCard, and American Express."

Carlo pulled a wallet from the inner pocket of his bomber jacket, and handed her a Visa card. She ran it through the terminal on her desk, watching him silently. Straight black hair fell like water past her shoulders. Her cheekbones were high and sharp, leaving her eyes in shadowed hollows. She looked like something out of some Native American version of the Old Testament, humorless and severe and bloodthirsty. She was a six foot tall, pure-blooded Navajo who knew nothing about being an Indian and everything about being a private investigator. In a city with over four thousand licensed detectives, Terminal Sue was, as she frequently told her clients, the *best*.

The small gray box on her desk spat out a scrap of paper. Terminal Sue ripped it out of the terminal and handed it to the man across from her. "Sign at the bottom."

Carlo van Zandt hesitated for an instant. "If you don't take my case, how do I get my nine hundred and thirty-five dollars back?"

Terminal Sue said, "Trust me. All relationships are based on trust." She'd read that once.

Carlo signed.

Terminal Sue smiled at him again. She always smiled when people gave her money. It was good business. "Now tell me about your chick."

"I'm being followed," Carlo blurted. "By some blond-haired chick."

"Wear looser pants," Terminal Sue suggested.

"It's been going on for almost a month now. At first I thought she was just, you know, like a fan. But –"

"You're a singer?"

"A musician," Carlo corrected. "I do more than sing."

"Right."

"The first time I noticed this chick, I was doing a gig at this club, *The Rock*. She followed me home that night, but I had someone with me already. So I didn't stop and give her directions."

Terminal Sue said, "Right."

"But she was keeping up pretty good anyway. I wasn't trying to lose her or anything, I figured if she made it all the way back to my place I'd invite her in."

"What would your date have thought about that?"

Carlo stared at her blankly. "What?"

Terminal Sue said, "Right."

"I live on Sunset. A couple of miles east of the beach. She followed me all the way to my house, but then when I stopped, she kept going." Carlo shrugged. "And I was like, cool. I already had one chick, I didn't need another one. But then a few days later I saw her again when I went to get groceries. And I was like, cool. Because I didn't have anybody with me, and I figured, why not. You know?"

Terminal Sue said, "If we could start this story closer to the end it would help."

Carlo looked hurt. "Okay. So yesterday, somebody searched my house. And I could tell, cause like, my stuff was moved. And then last night the blond chick followed me home again, from a gig over in Venice, and I stopped the car down on PCH at a light and got out to talk to her, cause I was starting to get pissed off about it all, and she tried to run me down." Carlo looked earnestly at Terminal Sue. "I think maybe we have like, a fatal attraction thing going on here."

Terminal Sue had been listening to the way he talked. She said, "Are you from the Valley?"

"I'm from Topeka."

"Topeka? Topeka, Kansas? Like Dorothy?"

"Dorothy wasn't from Topeka."

"I never met anybody from Kansas before. Although I knew people lived there," Terminal Sue added.

"My family lives there," said Carlo.

"But not Dorothy."

"I have a cousin named Dorothy."

"Does she have a dog named Toto?"

Carlo looked at Terminal Sue uncertainly. "Is that a joke?"

Terminal Sue stared at him. "I don't have a sense of humor. If you remember that we'll get along *much* better."

"Oh." Carlo was silent for a moment. "No. She doesn't have a dog named Toto."

"So you don't know who this blond woman is?"

"No."

"You've never seen her except when she was following you?"

"I don't think so. But you know – blond chicks all kinda look alike. I think maybe she was in the audience that first night, when I played *The Rock*."

"I understand the problem," Terminal Sue said.

Carlo looked relieved.

"What would you like me to *do* about it?"

"Make her stop following me."

"Do you want me to find out *why* she's following you?"

"Do I have to pay extra for that?"

"No."

Carlo thought about it. "Yeah," he decided. "I'd like to know why she's following me. But even more important –"

"Yes?"

"I'd like to know why she tried to run me over."

"Of course." Terminal Sue nodded. "Perfectly natural under the circumstances."

"It won't cost extra?"

"All part of the service." Terminal Sue picked up the charge slip, handed Carlo the yellow copy and tucked the white away in a drawer. "The clock started when you walked in here. I suggest you leave now."

A flash of panic crossed Carlo's face. "Why?"

Terminal Sue said, "She can't follow you while you're sitting in my office. Can she?"

"I guess not." Carlo rose and headed reluctantly toward the door.

"A piece of advice," Terminal Sue said.

Carlo turned back in the doorway.

"Take the bandanna off."

As the door swung shut behind Carlo, Terminal Sue walked into the back room and got her Nikon off the shelf. With no particular hurry, she jacked a new roll of film into the chamber, took off the medium distance lens and put on the telephoto lens. She walked back out into the main office, to the window overlooking the parking lot. She snapped two photos of Carlo as he was getting into the Miata, a third photo of the Miata itself, with its license plate clearly visible. The Miata pulled much too quickly out of the lot, onto Sunset, bouncing over the speed bumps.

Terminal Sue waited, standing patiently with the camera still up to her eye.

A gray Mercedes Benz pulled out of a parking space ten down from the spot where Carlo had been parked. She started the auto advance and tracked the car as it pulled out of the parking lot, and into traffic on Sunset.

She got half a dozen good shots of a middle-aged blond guy in the Mercedes.

Bogie Freedom

BEHIND THE BAR at *The Rock* hung a large, professionally printed placard. It said:

FOR BOOKING INFORMATION,

CONTACT BOGIE FREEDOM.

(213) 555-4273

Scrawled across the bottom in pencil were the words:

Leave a message on the answering machine, and maybe, if I want to talk to you, I'll call you back.

Below this, in red ink, were the words:

I probably don't want to talk to you.

A fifty foot bar dominated the room, with a small raised platform serving as a stage in the corner. Carlo looked at the tall bartender who stood, wiping glasses, behind the bar that the sign had been taped to. The bartender, Walkin' Talkin' Dave Bradden, smiled when Carlo came in, as if he were pleased to see him. Carlo didn't smile back. He wasn't fooled. Walkin' Talkin' Dave was an indiscriminate smiler who was pleased to see practically anyone. "Where's Bogie?"

Dave shrugged. "Around."

"Around where? I need to talk to him."

Dave returned his attention to his glasses. For no reason his smile became a grin. "Try in back."

IT WAS WEDNESDAY, and Bogie was in the back room pretending to be a detective. He didn't pretend to be a detective very often; he wasn't very good at it. He'd had a few cases, but he'd also had a tendency to hate his clients and sympathize with the people he was supposed to be investigating. His clients had an unfortunate tendency to hate Bogie back, and forget to pay him.

Sitting across from his client, Bogie thought it was a good thing he pretended to be an Entertainment Director at night. It paid regularly.

"You know," he said to the client who sat across from him, and who he was already beginning to hate, "I only do this because it gives me an excuse to hang around the bar all day and drink whiskey and play video games. I probably won't be of much help to you."

Carlo van Zandt stared at Bogie resentfully. He had never liked Bogie; Bogie pulled off with what appeared to be a complete lack of thought the style that Carlo had aspired to all his life, and managed only rarely. Bogie had a black fedora pulled low over his forehead, and a pony tail longer and blonder than Carlo's could ever hope to be. He wore a black suede and leather vest, black leather pants, black motorcycle boots, and a bright purple shirt with the sleeves rolled up.

Carlo had never seen him without his cheap black Dirty Harry sunglasses.

"But Bogie," Carlo whined, "Tom Rochester told me you'd be able to help me."

The fact that Carlo knew Tom made Bogie hate Carlo that much more. Tom Rochester had been the client in an unfortunately successful case, and he'd been telling people about Bogie ever since. Bogie was ready to kill him.

Bogie checked his watch. "Look," he said, "it's 3:42. You've got until exactly 3:55 to tell me what the problem is. That gives me five minutes to tell you I can't help you. And you do realize that in only five minutes I won't be able to let you down easily?" He spared Carlo a concerned glance. "This isn't going to be pleasant. Are you sure you want to go through with it?"

Carlo was a half-bright white-trash rock and roll singer, and Bogie knew they were easily confused; Carlo said, "What?"

Bogie sighed. "All right. It's 3:43. Say what you came to say. But it's all your fault. No one told you to come in this close to four o'clock."

"Some chick's following me," Carlo blurted.

"Why?" Bogie asked.

"I don't *know*. She's just after me."

Bogie leaned back in his chair, and said soothingly, in the voice he used when he pretended to be a minister, "Tell me about it. Tell me the whole sordid story."

"You remember last time I played here, when –"

"When your drummer threw up on his drums during a song and kept trying to play? And the vomit was flying everywhere? Yeah, I remember."

Carlo winced. "That time. Anyway, I was leaving that night, and this blond chick in a blue BMW tried to follow me home. Except I think she did follow me home."

"Did you invite her in?"

"No."

"I'd have invited her in," Bogie told him. "Then you'd know who she was and why she was following you. And you wouldn't need me."

Carlo looked at Bogie sullenly, wanting to tell him that he *didn't* need him, that he already had some Indian chick looking into this for him. But Carlo suspected that maybe he really did need Bogie.

He and Bogie came from the same world. They spoke the same language. Bogie, Carlo knew, would never ask him if his cousin Dorothy had a dog named Toto. And if he did it would be a joke, and they could laugh about it together.

Carlo took a deep breath, and recapped the entire sequence of events for Bogie. "And then last night, when I was leaving *UnClean Joe's*, down in Venice Beach, she followed me again. And when I stopped the car up on PCH, at the California Incline, she tried to run me over."

"*Damn*," Bogie said, "That's *illegal*." He paused. "Well, I guess it's not illegal if you stop afterwards. Only if you run over them and then run away. Did you call the police?"

Walkin' Talkin' Dave came into the back room and took Bogie's glass of whiskey. "3:58 and counting, Bogie."

Bogie turned back to Carlo. "I'm sorry, but you've taken up some of my minutes, and now my refusal's not only going to be harsh, it's going to be abrupt. No."

"But —"

"*Hell* no."

"Can't we talk about this?" Carlo asked.

"3:59," Walkin' Talkin' Dave called out.

Bogie sighed. "You're going to have to come back and let me turn you down tomorrow, Carlo. I'm out of time." Bogie stood up and turned away.

"But Bogie, I *need* your help."

Bogie stood in the doorway leading to the bar. "I'm sorry, Carlo, but I'm done being a detective for the day. I'm being the Entertainment Director now." He looked at Carlo pityingly. "I wasn't really planning on being a detective tomorrow, but if you come back early we can talk about this some more, and I'll let you down gently, okay?" He turned his back on Carlo and went out into the bar. He thought maybe if he pretended the other man wasn't there he'd go away quietly.

He slid onto a barstool. Walkin' Talkin' Dave Bradden filled a glass almost to the rim with white rum, and then added a splash of pineapple juice, and topped it with a cherry, a slice of orange, and a small pink umbrella. "What's Carlo want?"

Bogie shook his head. "I don't know. We didn't get that far. He'll tell me tomorrow, and after I turn him down, if you still want to know, you can ask me. And then I'll tell you. Okay?"

Walkin' Talkin' Dave smiled at Bogie, showing a row of impressively even white teeth. "Sure thing, Bogie."

Bogie smiled back, because unlike Carlo, he believed that all of the smiles Dave aimed at him were intended for him.

Bogie took a sip of the rum with a splash of pineapple juice. Entertainment Directors drank rum with a splash of pineapple juice. With little umbrellas in them. Detectives drank whiskey, straight. "I've got to get out of the detective business," he confided to Walkin' Talkin' Dave. "I hate all my clients, and I don't like the whiskey much better."

Carlo settled himself onto the stool beside Bogie. "I'll pay you in advance."

Bogie looked straight ahead, so he wouldn't have to look at Carlo. It didn't work; Carlo stared back at him from the mirror behind the bar. "I'm being the Entertainment Director, man. If you want a gig, say so. Otherwise buzz off."

"Okay. I want a gig."

"I'm booked," Bogie snapped.

"You check out the blond chick and I'll play Sunday night. I've got a following, Bogie. I'll bring people in." Carlo leaned close to Bogie and said slyly, "Blue Hair'll like that."

"Leave Blue Hair out of this!" said Bogie sharply. "I'm the Entertainment Director, and what I say goes. Don't *ever* forget that."

"Hey, Dave," said Carlo, "seen Blue Hair?"

"She was in earlier. She'll be back."

Carlo said, "I'll wait. Give me a Bud."

Walkin' Talkin' Dave placed a Long-Necked Budweiser on the bar in front of Carlo, and walked away.

An uncomfortable silence descended. Bogie, as the Entertainment Director, and Walkin' Talkin' Dave, as the Bar Manager, supposedly ran *The Rock*. But everybody knew that in reality, Blue Hair, the extremely old woman who owned the club, had them both crushed under her heel.

Bogie said, "Every Sunday night until January."

Carlo could not contain his outrage at the suggestion. "Are you out of your fuckin' mind? I'm an *artist*. I've got a *record* deal."

Bogie snorted. "Fine. Get run over."

"Look, I *can't,* man. That's too long. But I'll work –" Carlo paused, thinking. "Two months of Sundays, okay? Through August."

"Four months," Bogie said. "Through Halloween. *And* you pay me in advance."

"How much?"

"How much do you have?"

Carlo searched his pockets, came out with a crumpled wad of bills. He straightened them out on the bartop, counting. "Eighteen, twenty, twenty . . . four. Twenty-four dollars." He looked at Bogie sharply. "Am I getting *paid* for these Sunday nights?"

"Of course not."

"Then why do I have to pay you? This is an even trade, right?"

"As the Entertainment Director," said Bogie evenly, "you and I have concluded a business arrangement whereby you perform in my club, gaining exposure for yourself, and entertaining my customers. We both benefit. It is a mutually profitable arrangement. Is this clear?"

"Well, yeah, but –"

Bogie could feel himself warming to the subject. "As a Professional Detective, you are further retaining my services to determine the motives of the woman who has been following you, and who attempted to run you over on the Pacific Coast Highway after your gig at *UnClean Joe's* last night. Is it reasonable, I ask you, that I perform this service for you without charging?"

"Well –" Carlo said.

"I think that's my twenty-four dollars," said Bogie. He looked to Walkin' Talkin' Dave. "What do you think, Dave?"

Walkin' Talkin' Dave nodded. "I think that's your twenty-four dollars, too."

Bogie stared at Carlo with his sunglasses. "Any questions? Like, for example, When do you start on Sundays? Nine o'clock. Any further questions?"

"Yeah," Carlo said. "When do you start detecting?"

"Right now." Bogie took a sip of his rum and pineapple juice. "So get the hell out. I can't do it with you watching."

Carlo sighed and stood up; the Indian chick had said the same thing. Clearly he was among professionals. His Bud sat, untouched, in front of him, dripping sweat down the label and onto the pristine surface of the bar. He looked at Bogie anxiously. "You're serious. You're really going to look into this for me?"

Bogie Freedom said, "Yes."

Carlo backed toward the door. "I can *trust* you? You're not like the others?"

"Of course not," said Bogie soothingly. "Oh, and Carlo?"

Carlo looked at Bogie hopefully. "Yeah?"

"Lose the bandanna, man."

BOGIE TOOK A bar napkin and scribbled on it, "I, Carlo van Zandt, promise to appear on stage at *The Rock* every Sunday night at 9 p.m. until Halloween." Bogie forged Carlo's signature and the date at the bottom of the napkin. He chortled and rubbed his hands together. "Blue Hair'll really like this."

Walkin' Talkin' Dave nodded. "I imagine."

Detecting

BOGIE KNOCKED ON the door of Dreadful Sam's Sunset Boulevard house, a couple of miles up from the beach. The door had at some point been painted green, but the green paint was peeling off to reveal an alarming, yellow-tinged coat of something that had once perhaps been brown. Where the alarming yellow was peeling off, Bogie could see real wood.

A sign in the front yard, like the signs that realtors used to announce that a chunk of land that someone happened to claim to own was now for sale, said:

MAGIC

The sign always made Bogie want to take up "magic." It was so indefinite. Not "white magic" or "black magic" or even "Earth magic," which Bogie's ex-girlfriend Natasha had claimed to practice. Just good old-fashioned "magic."

Dreadful Sam answered the door in a black bathrobe. Dreadful Sam was six foot four and had piercing gray eyes that made Bogie feel guilty even when he hadn't done anything wrong. He was somewhere in his mid-fifties, as gaunt and hard-muscled as a victim of the Depression, as though he had dug ditches every day of his adult life. His wiry, jet-black hair was salted with the faintest touch of gray. He spoke in a voice as deep and authoritative as anything Bogie had ever heard on Channel 2 Action News. "Good morning, Bogie. I've got tea brewing. Come in."

Bogie followed Dreadful Sam back through the outer parlor, with the long, scarred black table where Dreadful Sam talked to customers, back into the old, cluttered house itself. Dreadful Sam owned things that Bogie had never seen anywhere else, things that were beautiful and ugly, illegal and immoral. They needed dusting and Bogie coveted them all, particularly the baby's skull, and the ivory mask it was propped on.

Dreadful Sam led Bogie into the kitchen, where Bogie suspected the man actually *did* the magic. Something about the way the place smelled. It was neither a bad odor nor a good odor, but if he breathed the air in the kitchen too deeply, too long, Bogie had visions. The first time he'd visited Dreadful Sam, before he had learned the dangers of lengthy visits, Bogie had come back from a dream of his mother's death to find himself sitting at Dreadful Sam's kitchen table, tea cup cold in his hand, and it had been a long time before Bogie returned.

A pair of cups were set on the kitchen table. The yellow print curtains were drawn back, letting the early morning sunshine into the room. Dreadful Sam gestured to Bogie to sit, and poured tea from a small, pale blue stone teapot into Bogie's cup.

Bogie lifted the cup, holding it close so he could inhale the steam. "Licorice." It did not even occur to Bogie to ask Dreadful Sam how he had known to put out a second cup.

Dreadful Sam poured for himself, and then sat opposite Bogie. "What's wrong?"

"What do you mean?" asked Bogie quickly. "Why should anything be wrong?"

"The only time you ever come and visit me," said Dreadful Sam, deep voice rumbling in his chest like the threat of the Earth itself, "is when you have a problem."

"That's a lie." Dreadful Sam just looked at Bogie. "Not that I'm *calling* you a liar, mind you," Bogie continued. "But I've come to see you on . . . *numerous* occasions when nothing was wrong."

Dreadful Sam's steady gaze did not waver.

"Okay," said Bogie. "So I have a small problem. But it's just a little one. Inconsequential. You know Carlo van Zandt?"

"He lives down the street."

Bogie smiled in relief. "You do know him."

"Not well. I know he rents a house down the street. He tried to have me tell his fortune once."

"Well, he says some blond ch – blond woman is following him. I don't suppose you've seen any blond women around?"

Dreadful Sam shook his head *no*. "This is L.A., Bogie. Where would I see blond women?"

"This particular blond woman's in a blue BMW. Have you seen any blue BMWs around?"

Dreadful Sam said gently, "Bogie, are you being a detective again?"

"Maybe."

"Do you remember when those people shot at you, Bogie?"

"No."

"And the time you spent six hours chained to a bench at the West Hollywood police station, and nobody would come bail you out?"

Bogie shook his head. "I don't remember that either."

"Being a detective isn't *safe,* Bogie. There are other things you can be. Weren't you a jet pilot for a while?"

"I was a helicopter pilot. And I crashed the helicopter. I *do* remember that."

"And a priest. Weren't you a priest for a while?"

Bogie stared at Dreadful Sam sullenly. "Do you know what they expect from priests? The things you have to give up?"

Dreadful Sam nodded. "I've heard. But they don't get shot at. And they hardly ever get chained to benches in the West Hollywood police station."

"Look, this isn't really detective work. It's, it's, snooping. For a friend. For Carlo, my friend. He's being followed."

A flicker of interest crossed Dreadful Sam's features. "By a blond woman in a BMW?"

"Yeah. So, like, if you could kind of keep an eye on him? He's right down the street, and you never go anywhere anyway."

Dreadful Sam's manner and expression did not change. "And what makes you think that?"

"You're always here when I come to see you."

Dreadful Sam said, "I always know when you're coming."

AFTER LEAVING DREADFUL Sam's kitchen, Bogie headed out to *UnClean Joe's* to do some more detecting.

A bouncer who was meaner, taller, and had more scars than the bouncers employed at *The Rock* greeted Bogie at the door. "Hey, Bogie." His voice was high and sweet, complemented by a guileless smile and green eyes the color of nothing ever seen indoors.

"Hey, Bubba." Bogie smiled almost as sweetly as the bouncer. He liked Bubba. Some day UnClean Joe was going to make the wrong move, and Bubba would be the bouncer at *The Rock*.

"What brings you by? Trolling for talent?"

Bogie shook his head. "Nope. We have all the talent we need. We even have Carlo van Zandt playing Sundays."

"No shit? Sundays?" Bubba looked impressed.

"Every Sunday till Halloween," said Bogie, and went inside.

UNCLEAN JOE'S WAS a hotbed of illegal drugs, up and coming rock stars, and groupies with every disease known to man and a few that hadn't been catalogued yet. The stage along the back wall was larger than *The Rock*'s stage, the bar was smaller, and the bottles behind the bar had labels that bore no obvious relationship to the liquid inside.

Bogie settled down at one of the dirty tables. He brushed some unnamable filth off the chair before he sat in it. A prostitute-groupie-waitress Bogie had fired from *The Rock* two years ago appeared beside the table. Her weary, fuck-you smile faded when she saw Bogie. "What are you here for?"

"Lunch," said Bogie. "What's good?"

The waitress snorted. "Are you serious?"

Bogie knew better than to order the spaghetti. Or the Mexican food, or anything that came in unidentifiable, mixed-together clumps – that included the salad and the sandwiches.

"I'll have a Diet Coke," said Bogie. "In the can."

The waitress disappeared and Bogie sat back in his chair and examined the people scattered through the club. It wasn't noon yet, so the lunch rush, such as it was, hadn't started. A handful of middle-aged, early morning alcoholics were gathered at the bar; the crowd got younger as the day got older. Two bikers sat together in a darkened corner, with the remains of half a dozen Long-Necked Bud Dry's on the table in front of them. In another corner a scrawny, long-haired, red-eyed man in a white cowboy hat hunched in patented misery over a plate of the spaghetti, poking at it suspiciously with a fork.

Bogie said, "Rex? Hey, Rex! Here boy!"

The red-eyed drunk looked up. "Are you mocking me?"

"Rex? Rex O'Herlihan? Is that you?"

The drunk peered at Bogie. "Yeah. Bogie? Bogie Freedom? Where the hell have you been?" Rex eased his way carefully out of his chair, glanced around to see if anybody was watching him, and walked toward Bogie with the steady, even gate of a practiced drunk. Halfway to Bogie's table, he halted dead in his tracks, turned toward the waitress who was getting Bogie's Diet Coke, and hollered, "Hey!"

The girl looked up.

"You see that spaghetti?" Rex pointed at the spaghetti. "Don't touch that spaghetti. I'm eating it." He made his way to Bogie's table, setting down across from him. He sighed heavily and said, "There's human hair in that spaghetti."

"And you're eating it," Bogie said.

Rex shrugged. "I've had worse. So –"

Bogie smiled at Rex. "Yes."

"You wanna know what's going on here?"

It was the reason Bogie had come to *UnClean Joe's;* Rex was the only drunk Bogie knew who offered to tell people what was going on if they would buy him a drink. He was an invaluable detecting resource.

"I'm looking for somebody," Bogie said. "A blond chick."

It took Rex a long moment to work through the thought. "Any blond chick? Or a particular blond chick?"

"A particular one."

Rex shook his head mournfully. "All blond chicks look alike."

Bogie nodded. He had often thought it was true. "Well, this one's been following Carlo van Zandt around. She was here night before last."

"Ah." Rex's red eyes gleamed unnaturally. "*That* blond chick. There's more than one, you know. As a matter of fact, there's a few blond dudes." Rex leaned close to Bogie and whispered, "They come out of the North."

TERMINAL SUE FINISHED reading Carlo's TRW report while working her way through her takeout Mexican lunch. Normally the restaurant across the street did not deliver, but Terminal Sue could be persuasive when she wanted to be; arranging that her lunches get delivered hadn't even required her to threaten anyone. She was rather proud of that.

Carlo van Zandt, according to his TRW report, was usually on time with his car payments, except for last Christmas when he'd missed the entire month and made a double payment in January. He had no other significant credit record, except his Visa card, which he paid regularly.

The DMV printouts were more telling. He had been cited four times for Exhibition of Speed; one DUI, over four years old. He'd been involved in a fender-bender two years back. Not a year had passed in the last five when he hadn't been in danger of having his license revoked for excessive moving violations. In addition to the Exhibition of Speed tickets he had half a dozen simple speed limit infractions, and an illegal U-turn.

The Miata was registered in what Terminal Sue assumed was his mother's name, Marina van Zandt.

Beyond his credit and driving records, Terminal Sue could find no public information on Carlo. He had never been a member of the Armed Forces. He didn't have a police record, and Terminal Sue wasn't interested in his school records, not if she had to call Topeka to get them.

The gray Mercedes Benz, license plate 2HPW417, was registered to Fourth Kingdom Import, Inc., in Anaheim, Orange County. There were no tickets on it.

Terminal Sue tapped her speakerphone on. She punched (714) 555-1212.

"Operator 431. What city, please?"

"Anaheim. A business, Fourth Kingdom Import."

"One moment . . ." Keyboard sounds from the other end of the line. "There is no listing for that company."

"Didn't really expect one." Terminal Sue thanked the operator and tapped the *off* button. She threw the remains of her lunch in the wastebasket by the desk, locked up the office, and headed for Carlo's house.

With any luck, he wouldn't be home.

TERMINAL SUE PARKED her late-model black Mustang down the street from Carlo's house, not far from the house where Dreadful Sam had spent the last thirty-five years telling fortunes. She thought about stopping by, but she was working, and there was a customer's car parked in Dreadful Sam's driveway, a gray Honda.

She didn't like driving the Mustang; for all its reputation as a muscle car its pickup was only fair. She owned two other sports cars and both of them blew Mustangs off the street. The Mustang handled poorly on curves and ate gas like nobody's business. But it was the cheapest real sports car you could buy, and there were so many of them in Los Angeles that nobody ever gave it a second glance.

Terminal Sue crossed Sunset and walked up the driveway to the front door. She stood at the door for a moment, listening. Someone inside. She knocked once, sharply, and then stood slightly to the side of the door.

The noise stopped instantly. A moment later a blond man wearing a black fedora and a pair of cheap black Ray-Ban knockoffs answered the door. He was a handsomer version of Carlo, same height, weight, and build, but with better features and a more alert expression. "Yeah?"

Terminal Sue said, "Is Carlo here?"

"No," Bogie Freedom said, "definitely not." He started to close the door.

Terminal Sue put her foot in the crack. "Do you live here?"

"No, definitely not." Bogie paused. "Would you take your foot out of the door, please?"

Terminal Sue shook her head. "No. Definitely not."

They stood on opposite sides of the doorway, looking at each other through the crack. Terminal Sue heard a car pull up to the curb behind her; without taking her foot out of the door she glanced around and saw a blond man and a blond woman stepping from the gray Mercedes Benz. A blue BMW, carrying two blond men, pulled up immediately behind the gray car.

Bogie said, "Well. Blond people."

Terminal Sue looked at him suspiciously. "You're blond."

"Yeah? So what –" Without finishing the sentence, Bogie opened the door wide, grabbed Terminal Sue by the upper arm, yanked her inside and slammed the front door. He snapped the deadbolt shut, blinked and looked down at the object jammed into his belly-button. "What's that?"

"That," said Terminal Sue, "is a Ruger 9mm BlackHawk. My gun."

"So? I've got a gun."

Terminal Sue looked at him coldly.

"Well," Bogie said, "I could *get* a gun if I wanted to."

Someone knocked on the front door. A deep male voice said, "Carlo! We need to talk, Carlo! I have a gig for you!"

Terminal Sue took the house in at a glance. It was a pit. There were twenty or thirty Taco Bell and Jack-in-the-Box bags scattered around, and the place reeked of old hot sauce and tortillas. Plates crusted with what had once doubtless been organic material were scattered throughout the living room, piled three and four high. Glasses of some unidentifiable brown liquid, with pale green mold growing in them, sprouted on the console television set, from the bookshelf the stereo sat on, and on the stained, ragged couch. Dirty clothing covered the floor like a colorful carpet. Three ashtrays were filled to overflowing; small bowls had been used after the ashtrays filled up. Terminal Sue thought she had never seen more cigarette butts in one place in her life.

"Carlo!" the man bellowed. "Open up, damn it. It's me, Klaus!"

Bogie said, "This is where I run away." He glanced down at the gun Terminal Sue still had jammed in his ribs. "Do you mind?"

Terminal Sue pulled the gun away from his ribs. "A little." She trailed Bogie through the piled trash in the living room, and into the kitchen. The rear door was a solid block of wood, without a peephole or window; Terminal Sue saw the handle jiggle as Bogie reached for it. She grabbed him by the neck of his shirt, pulled him back, and fired four times into the door, aiming high, to upset whoever was standing on the other side. The door was locked from the inside; she unlocked it, stood to the side and swung it open. Nobody visible from this angle; she stuck her hand outside the door and fired four more shots into the backyard, fanning out.

"Are you out of your fucking mind?" Bogie stared at her. "You could *kill* somebody."

"I don't kill people by accident." Terminal Sue lunged through the open door, into the small backyard, and hit the ground rolling. She came to her feet with the gun up, walking backward: the backyard was lined with a white picket fence of all goddamn things, and someone blond was running away from her, around the side of the house, probably the person who'd been trying to open the door. Terminal Sue fired twice, trailing the moving shape, to encourage whoever it was to keep moving.

Bogie Freedom ran by Terminal Sue without speaking, heading for the small gate at the rear of the yard, letting out onto the alleyway behind the house. Terminal Sue ignored him; she walked backward, Ruger at ready, watching both sides of the house, until she reached the gate, and then hopped the fence. The alleyway stretched away for a block in either direction, and the man in the fedora was nowhere to be seen.

She glanced back at the house; nothing. Silence.

Terminal Sue kicked the clip free, put the spare in, and tucked the clip, with four shots still left in it, into her pants pocket. She headed at a sprint down the alleyway to the spot, two blocks west, where her car was parked.

Ten Percent

AT 4:32 A.M., Carlo van Zandt pulled into the driveway of his Sunset Boulevard house and killed the engine. It was as quiet as it ever got along Sunset Boulevard; only the preponderance of Jags and Porsches and other exotics, and the fact that most of the traffic was doing better than fifty on a city street, let Carlo know that he wasn't at home in Topeka, Kansas.

As far as he could tell, nobody had followed him home tonight. It was encouraging; maybe the blond chick had finally given up on it.

The light was on in his kitchen. Carlo struggled to remember if he'd left it on. He hoped Janie wasn't waiting for him inside; even if he hadn't been drinking through most of his last set, he doubted if he'd have been able to remember whether he'd given her a key. He'd said he was going to, but didn't remember if he had.

Carlo sat motionless in the car for a long moment. It was weird, but he felt as though he were being watched. He pulled his Fender Stratocaster from the passenger seat, got out of the Miata and looked around. Nothing out of the ordinary – well, the lights were on at the house of the wizard who lived down the street, but aside from that nothing unusual seemed to be going on.

Carlo frowned, staring at the wizard's house. *All* of the lights were on, every one, from the little light that illuminated the sign that said MAGIC, to the lights in the little turrets on the second floor. Gables, he thought they were called. The downstairs lights were on, glowing bright in the windows, and for a moment Carlo was tempted to wander on over and see if Dreadful Sam was awake. He'd tried to get Dreadful Sam to tell him his fortune once, and Dreadful Sam had refused to take his money. Maybe if he went over *tonight* Dreadful Sam would tell his fortune.

Somehow, though, even though the house was lit up like the model home in a new real estate development, it didn't look friendly at all. There were bad vibes coming out of the wizard's house.

Carlo shook his head and went inside.

SOMEONE HAD BEEN in his place again.

That was the first thing Carlo noticed after flipping the light switch in the living room. The Taco Bell and Jack-in-the-Box bags were scattered around the living room floor in a different pattern than the one in which he'd left them. And two of the bowls of cigarette butts were scattered across the floor; Carlo *never* kicked over the cigarette butts.

Two messages blinked on his answering machine. Carlo ignored them; he set the Stratocaster in the corner, leaning it carefully against the wall, in the one clean spot in the entire living room. He made his way toward the kitchen, stepping over and around piles of trash; halfway there he knew who he would find inside.

Klaus Vodd sat at Carlo's kitchen table, smoking and drinking Lipton Instant Iced Tea out of a can. Beside him sat the blond chick who'd been following Carlo.

Carlo stopped dead in his tracks. He very nearly hated Klaus Vodd. Six weeks ago the man had introduced himself to Carlo, after a gig at *The Rock*. He'd claimed to be an agent, but six weeks later Carlo was starting to have his doubts. If Klaus had another client, Carlo didn't know about it. In six weeks he hadn't done anything for Carlo that Carlo couldn't have done more cheaply for himself. He'd gotten Carlo bookings at clubs Carlo had played before; had failed to deliver on his promise to get Carlo even looked at by one of the major record companies. For the last six weeks the man had stolen ten percent of everything Klaus made, even the two gigs Carlo had lined up himself; if Klaus knew about it, Klaus got his. "How did you get in?" Carlo asked. "And where did you find this chick? She's the one who's been following me."

Klaus took a long drag on his cigar before answering. Klaus was a gray-haired man with pale blue eyes, stocky and muscular. He looked like a wrestler gone slightly to seed, with a little pot belly helping to disguise the physique of an ex-Mister Olympia. He wore thin horn-rimmed glasses and smoked the cheapest, smelliest cigars Carlo had ever encountered.

The woman next to him looked cold as ice.

Klaus blew smoke at Carlo and said, "The door was open."

"No it wasn't," Carlo said. "I always lock my door." He sneered at Klaus. "We're not in Kansas anymore, Toto." He walked past Klaus to the refrigerator, opened the door and gazed into the empty expanse. He thought with some satisfaction that now he could fire both Bogie and the Indian, now that he'd found the blond chick himself.

Out of the corner of his eye Carlo could see the blond chick getting out of her chair. She said, "We've got to do something about getting you a maid, Adolph."

A streak of fire touched the side of Carlo's neck. Bright red splattered against the far wall of the refrigerator, and Carlo leaned forward to see what it was, and kept leaning; suddenly his muscles would not hold him upright. He had never even heard the first shot; he heard the second, and the third. They were loud, fucking bombs bursting in air. Two sledgehammer blows, one after the other, struck Carlo high on his back, and he went down to his knees, hands grasping at the sides of the refrigerator.

Something hot and metallic touched him at the back of his skull.

Klaus Vodd, still sitting in his chair, smoking, watching, said politely, "You can keep all of this one."

ACROSS THE STREET, Dreadful Sam sat alone in his kitchen drinking orange spice tea. He could see Carlo in his mind's eye. The black aura around Carlo faded slowly, but shortly before dawn it was gone.

When Carlo was dead, Dreadful Sam rose slowly to his feet. He wandered through his house, and one by one, turned the lights off.

AT 8:15 A.M., Terminal Sue called Carlo. The phone rang once and was answered by a male voice she did not recognize. "Hello?"

Terminal Sue hung up quickly.

"HUNG UP," SAID Sergeant Joe Donnelley. "Third one this morning."

Detective Rocco Dennison said, "Crap." He wasn't talking about the hangups; he was talking about Joe Donnelley. He despised Joe Donnelley. Fucking flat footed Irish, they gave the police department a bad name. And now they were taking over the phone book business.

Rocco Dennison was a short, stout police officer of Italian descent, with a receding hairline and beady little eyes that saw more than they ought to, mostly of the wrong things.

Rocco kicked at a pile of Taco Bell bags. He sort of liked Taco Bell. But this musician's house was putting him off. If you'd asked him this morning if he could have gone for a tostada, he'd have said, yeah, sure. But you can only look so many half-eaten tostadas in the eye before you start to lose your appetite.

Burritos, now, burritos were nicely wrapped up, self-contained, and if something was growing inside them, you couldn't tell. You could sure tell that stuff was growing on the tostadas. It sprouted up like a miniature forest, full of miniature lions and tigers and bears, oh my.

Well, actually they were ants and cockroaches.

Rocco refused to even look at the bean dip.

Joe Donnelley said, "Have you noticed the mold all over these half eaten Jack in the Box hamburgers?"

"Yeah," said Rocco. "I wish he'd stuck to tacos."

"Yeah," Donnelley agreed. "Those burger buns *really* display the mold."

Rocco ignored him. He rewound the cassette and listened to it again.

Beep. It was a man's voice. "I've been looking into your chick problem, man. There really is a problem . . . and I thought you were just goofy. I'll tell you all about it on Sunday. I'm doing my part, you better be there."

Beep. A woman's voice. "Carlo, this is Susan Walks-Far. Stop by my office. We have things to discuss."

Rocco felt a little better after having listened to the tape. The man was some rock and roll creep, you could hear it in his voice. And the woman, he had the woman's name.

How many Susan Walks-Fars could there be in the city of Los Angeles?

THERE WERE TWO.

Susan Walks-Far was a middle-aged Indian woman with black hair and black eyes who looked at Rocco as though she wanted to tie him to an ant hill and pour honey on him. She bounced a baby on one knee as they talked. "You want a cup of coffee?" she asked.

If he took the coffee, what would be in it? But if he refused the coffee, it might offend her. "Sure," he said, "sure I'd like some coffee." Thank God she hadn't offered him a tostada. Rocco was afraid of the woman, and of the baby on her knee. It kept staring at him.

They sat in the woman's overly clean kitchen. You could tell the kitchen was used only because things were worn. The tile floor had been scrubbed until the tile markings had almost worn off. The cleanliness was almost frightening, after Carlo's house.

There was no telephone. It was why Rocco was sitting in the middle of this woman's kitchen, rather than having called her to see if she was the Susan Walks-Far he wanted. The computer check he'd run had supplied him with the name and addresses of two Susan Walks-Fars. One of them was a private detective, and nobody had answered *her* phone all morning. Joe Donnelley was sitting outside her office right now, waiting to see if she showed up.

This Susan Walks-Far, much to Rocco's disappointment, did not have the same voice as the Susan Walks-Far on the answering machine.

The woman chased half a dozen children out of the kitchen upon Rocco's arrival, children ranging in age from toddlers to teenagers.

"You want some honey in that coffee?"

Rocco made a little yelping noise.

The woman frowned at him. "Is that a no?"

"I'm investigating a murder," Rocco blurted.

"I don't know anything about any murderers," the woman said. "I don't even know any dead people. People in my family live a really, really long time. It's the food," she said. "We eat good food. Burritos, tostadas. Lots of corn. If you want to stay for lunch –"

Rocco said quickly, "Do you know a Carlo van Zandt?"

"Is he dead? I told you, I don't know no dead people."

"Yes," said Rocco. "He's been murdered."

"All murdered people are dead, and I told –"

"Yeah, yeah," said Rocco. "You don't know no dead people." Rocco, a twenty-six year veteran of the homicide department, wished he didn't know any dead people. "Do you know another Susan Walks-Far?"

"Sure," said Susan Walks-Far. "I know a Susan Walks-Far." She smiled at him, a flash of white teeth in the dark Indian features, and then her eyes slipped slightly to one side. "But she doesn't know any dead people either."

Rocco knew she was lying. She didn't lie well. Apparently she hadn't had much practice at it. He supposed anybody with as many children as she had didn't need to lie, they only needed to holler. Rocco, who had no children, recalled his own childhood. It had involved a lot of hollering. "We're looking for this other Susan Walks-Far, ma'am. You know where I could find her?"

"No, no," said Susan Walks-Far immediately. "I never see her. She never comes to visit."

"Your daughter?"

The woman nodded. "Ungrateful," she said.

THE UNIFORMED OFFICER who had been working the stretch of Sunset around Carlos's house knocked on what felt like the thousandth door.

He got a splinter in his knuckle.

The door swung open, and a dreadful looking man said, "Yes?"

The cop stared at him. He wasn't sure why the man appeared dreadful. He wasn't ugly; he was simply . . . dire. Looking at him, the skin on the back of the cop's neck prickled into goose bumps.

ROCCO DENNISON SAID, "Mr. Sam?"

Dreadful Sam said, "Call me Dreadful."

This case was really beginning to bother Rocco. "All right," he said. "If that's what you want."

"It's my name," Dreadful Sam explained. "A friend gave it to me."

"Of course," Rocco agreed. "So you saw a murder."

"Yes."

"You were in Carlo's house?"

"No. I was right here at my kitchen table. Drinking tea. Orange spice. Would you like some?"

"No," said Rocco shortly. "I have an upset stomach. And you're not helping. You watched this murder from your kitchen table?"

The man simply looked at him with those colorless gray eyes. "Yes. That's right."

"MS. WALKS-FAR?"

"Yes?"

"Detective Dennison, ma'am." He flashed an LAPD badge at Terminal Sue, stowed it. "Homicide. May I have a moment of your time?"

Terminal Sue smiled a cold smile. "Of course." She led Detective Dennison into the inner office, gestured at the chair in front of her desk. "What can I do for you?"

"You haven't been in your office all day, Ms. Walks-Far."

"I've been busy."

Rocco nodded. "Of course. We're investigating the murder of Carlo van Zandt." Rocco paused, watching Terminal Sue.

Terminal Sue gazed back blandly.

Rocco waited.

Terminal Sue waited.

Rocco sighed. "He was murdered last night." Rocco paused again.

Terminal Sue waited.

"We recovered a answering machine cassette from his house, with a message from you on it."

Terminal Sue nodded. "Yes?"

"I take it you were working for him?"

"Yes."

"Would you mind telling me what your investigation involved?"

"Yes."

"Ms. Walks-Far, you do realize you could be arrested for obstruction of justice?"

Terminal Sue's cold smile reappeared. "Yes."

"Ms. Walks-Far, would you like to call your lawyer?"

"May I ask you a question?"

Rocco said with something like relief, "Yes."

"Am I a suspect in Mr. van Zandt's death?"

"At this point, no."

Terminal Sue said, "Carlo thought a blond woman was following him."

Rocco sighed again. "I knew it. Chick trouble."

Strangers In The Night

TERMINAL SUE PARKED her Mustang in a parking structure off of Sunset Boulevard and Highland, a half mile to the east of the last club that Carlo had played.

The Rock was a mid-size club at the corner of Sunset and Crescent Heights; Terminal Sue had never been inside it, but she'd been by often enough to see the crowds the place drew on weekend nights. She knew better than to try parking anywhere near it.

And she didn't mind walking.

Across the street from the club, the sound of the music drowned out the sound of the traffic. The lighted marquee hanging over the entrance said, in big letters:

> CARLO VAN ZANDT
>
> AND
>
> THE VAN ZANDT RAIDERS

In smaller letters, beneath that, it said:

AND BLEEDING CHROME TOO.

Sue crossed with the light; there were a couple dozen people waiting at the door, and she joined them.

The doorman was picking and choosing the clientele for the evening. "*You two wait,*" he shouted at a pair of longhairs in their early twenties. "*Too many guys inside already. If things even up later maybe we'll let you in.*" The doorman met Terminal Sue's eyes and looked away. He pointed to a pair of girls, dressed in black leather bras and skin-tight skirts. "*You're in.*" He didn't check their IDs.

Terminal Sue, dressed all in black, was not dressed appropriately for the club. She was wearing a shirt.

"*Excuse me*," shouted Terminal Sue at the doorman. "*I need to ask you a question.*"

The doorman shouted back, "*Yeah?*"

"*Who hires the musicians around here?*"

"*Bogie Freedom.*"

"*I need to see him.*"

The doorman shook his head. "*Bogie don't see no one without an appointment.*"

Terminal Sue edged close to the doorman. As he started to turn away from her, she grabbed his leather tie and pulled. When his eyes were even with hers she shouted, "*I have an appointment.*"

The music ceased abruptly; in the sudden silence the doorman's shout was incredibly loud. "*Got proof?*"

In a normal voice, Terminal Sue said, "No, but I got a gun."

"I can't let you go in there and kill Bogie."

"I could stay out here and kill you," Terminal Sue offered.

The doorman jerked his thumb at the doorway. "You're in."

A SECOND DOORMAN stood beyond the first doorman; he made Terminal Sue pay ten dollars before he'd let her past the entryway.

A sign at the entrance announced that the room's capacity was two hundred and fourteen persons; at least twice that many were packed into it. A tiny, empty dance floor sat up against one wall. The people who came to *The Rock* did not come to dance, and the music the speed metal band was playing didn't lend itself to dancing anyway. Terminal Sue could not remember having seen so much black leather in one place in her life. It looked like a herd of cows had exploded.

And the surplus of blond people made her uneasy. She'd never liked blondes much; recently she'd developed a real aversion to them.

Bleeding Chrome – three men and a spike-haired female guitar player – started up again as Terminal Sue entered. Terminal Sue listened to the song for a moment. She cocked her head, trying to make out the screamed lyrics. After a moment she turned, peering closely at the singer's mouth, trying to read his lips. There wasn't enough light, and she thought he was frothing a little anyway. The sound was a wall of white noise, loud and meaningless. Sue shrugged; she didn't care what he was singing about. She looked around the room, looking for anyone who looked as though they might work there. There didn't seem to be any cocktail servers; aside from the men at the door the only person she was certain worked there were the people behind the bar, three men and one woman. Terminal Sue fought her way through the crowd to the bar. A big guy in a cowboy hat leaned close to her and shouted, "*What can I get you, Chief?*"

Terminal Sue took her time answering. She looked the man over carefully. He was a couple of inches taller than her, maybe six-two, wearing cowboy boots and blue jeans. His hair was brown and shaggy, and he was tanned the color of old leather. He looked vaguely Indian to her. Following a slight lull in the music, Terminal Sue said, "Is that supposed to be a joke?"

The bartender smiled at her. "Sure. I'm a funny guy."

"I don't have a sense of humor," Terminal Sue informed him. "Is Bogie Freedom around?" She placed a twenty dollar bill on the counter.

The Indian cowboy bartender looked at the bill. "Not for twenty bucks he's not."

"How much would it take for him to show up?"

The bartender looked at her, unsmiling. "What do you want him for?"

"I need to ask him some questions, Chief. About Carlo van Zandt. And I need to do it before the police do."

The bartender looked her over carefully. "The police are going to come looking for Bogie? What did he do this time?"

"Is he here or not?"

A sudden blast of white noise music drowned out his reply. Terminal Sue shouted, *"Say again?"*

He pointed at a doorway toward the rear of the club. Terminal Sue reached for her twenty dollars. The bartender snatched it up quickly, smiled at her, and mouthed the word, *Mine.*

Terminal Sue mouthed back, *You're welcome.*

The bartender tucked the bill into his pocket and turned to another customer.

IT WAS QUIETER in the hallway that led toward the back, quiet enough that Terminal Sue could hear the distinctive sounds of a video game.

Two doors, along the length of the hallway, said *Us,* and *Them.* Terminal Sue hesitated, told herself she didn't care, and then pushed the *Us* door open anyway. It was a bathroom. She let the door closed and looked thoughtfully at the door marked *Them.*

It was probably just another bathroom. But what if it wasn't? What if it was something good, and she missed out on it? On the other hand, what if it was something bad? Maybe it was a door that led out into the alleyway behind the club, and then she wouldn't be able to get back in without threatening the doorman again.

Terminal Sue knew she didn't want to go through a doorway marked *Them.*

After a long moment she reached out with a hand, standing well back, and pushed it open anyway.

An alleyway.

Terminal Sue nodded and let the door swing shut. This was why she was the greatest detective in L.A.

In the back room, Bogie Freedom stood before a video game with a glowing sign that said *Space Nazis From Hell*. Bogie spun the ball with his right hand, punching a button with his left. The brightness control was set to max so he could see the screen through his cheap black sunglasses.

It was the man in the fedora, the man who had been at Carlo van Zandt's house the day before.

"Mr. Freedom?"

"Hang on." Bogie stared intently at the screen.

"Mr. Freedom, you need to speak to me."

"Could you hang on a sec?" Bogie glanced up at Terminal Sue just long enough for his last man to be garroted by a grinning, sadistic blond man in an SS uniform. Bogie stared at the screen in a rage. "*Now* look what you've done." He patted his pockets. "You got a quarter? I don't have a quarter."

"Mr. Freedom," Terminal Sue tried again.

Bogie looked up from the search of his pockets. "Look, I really think you owe me –" His voice trailed off. "You."

"Apparently," said Terminal Sue. She paused for effect and said, "How well do you know Carlo van Zandt?"

"*That* goddamn untrustworthy bandanna-wearing contract-breaking musical son of a bitch," Bogie said. "All I know is he's not here right now. What are you, a lawyer? Are you *his* lawyer?"

"No," Terminal Sue said. "I'm a detective."

"And I'm an Entertainment Director," Bogie sneered, "and that weaselly bastard Carlo's dust when I get my hands on him."

"You know people have been following Carlo?" asked Terminal Sue. "Blond people, like the blond people you ran away from yesterday?"

"Yeah? So what's your point?"

"Didn't you wonder, when Carlo didn't show up, what had happened to him?"

Bogie stared at her with his sunglasses. "*As the Entertainment Director, I know* what happened to him. He's drunk in Santa Barbara. At 2:31, when I am no longer the Entertainment Director, alternatives might occur to me."

"He's not in Santa Barbara. He's in the morgue."

Bogie's gaze shifted back to the video game. "Bummer." He rolled uselessly at the trackball, and mumbled, "Weaselly bastard." He turned back to Terminal Sue abruptly. "How about my quarter?"

"You can have a quarter, but –"

"Fine," Bogie interrupted. "Give it to me."

Terminal Sue took out a quarter and held it between her thumb and forefinger. "You need to speak with me once your game is over."

"Fine, fine," snapped Bogie. "Just give me the quarter and leave me alone until I've finished this game. And then I'll talk to you if I feel like it."

"And then you'll talk to me," said Terminal Sue. "Whether you feel like it or not."

Bogie stared morosely at the quarter she still held. He checked his pockets again, to make sure he hadn't missed anything.

BOGIE SAT DOWN across from her.

"Mr. Freedom –" she began.

"Call me Bogie," Bogie interrupted. "I don't plan on knowing you very long. But we may as well try to be friendly since we're sitting at the same table. Besides, I'm going to be mean to you in a few minutes, and maybe if we're on a first name basis you won't feel so bad about it."

Terminal Sue counted to five under her breath. When she looked up at Bogie again her features were very calm. "Okay. Bogie. Why are you planning on being mean to me?"

"Because," said Bogie, "whatever it is you want from me, I won't do it." Terminal Sue's lips parted as though she were about to speak, and Bogie added quickly, "No matter how trivial, I refuse."

"I don't want you to do anything. I need information. If –"

The dull, roaring sound of the music, a constant background noise which even in here had forced Terminal Sue to raise her voice to a near-shout to be heard, abruptly ceased.

Bogie Freedom frowned. "That's not how that song ends."

"You can tell the songs *apart*?"

"Hell, yes," said Bogie. "These guys are *artists*."

The brief silence was broken by high-pitched shrieks.

Bogie sighed. "Some chicks are fighting."

The door to Terminal Sue's left opened, and the tall, Indian-looking bartender stuck his head in. "Yo, Bogie. Wanna come take care of this?"

Bogie stood up. "I'll be back. Eventually. Don't feel obliged to wait."

Terminal Sue followed Bogie out into the main room. She stood in the doorway and watched Bogie watch the "chicks" battle up on the stage. One of the woman was about thirty, a tall spike-haired woman in silver spandex and long white coat – Bleeding Chrome's guitarist. Terminal Sue had seen her on the way in. She was down on the floor with a dark-haired girl in dark clothes who looked to be about sixteen. The older woman was winning; Sue supposed she'd had more experience at this sort of thing.

Terminal Sue shook her head in disgust and went back inside to wait.

After only a slight hesitation, she found herself standing in front of the *Space Nazis From Hell* game. She fished in her jeans for a quarter, came out with three and fed the first quarter into the game.

BOGIE GLANCED AWAY from the battling women, wondering if anyone had checked the younger one's ID. Where the hell were the bouncers, anyway? This was the sort of thing they got paid for, he knew. Bogie was not only the Entertainment Director, he was also by default the Head Bouncer. The last Head Bouncer had gone to jail for doing his job too well.

There was a loud thud, followed by an equally loud shriek, and Bogie looked back at the battle. The guitarist was bashing the dark-haired girl's skull against the dance floor. Bogie felt a surge of real alarm; a little fighting was one thing, but he didn't want cops showing up. "Hey!" he yelled. "Stop it. Stop it right now!" The guitarist *did* stop for a moment, looking around for the source of the voice. Bogie pushed the leather-clad audience out of his way and jumped up on the stage.

He grabbed the guitarist by her white coat. She belted him in the mouth. Bogie shoved her into the arms of the drummer, reached down and picked up the dazed girl lying on the floor. Blood trickled from a split lip and down the side of her temple.

She looked at Bogie appealingly.

"Miss," said Bogie sternly, "can I see your ID?"

THE FIRST GAME didn't last long. Terminal Sue wasn't entirely clear on the game's point. In Round One, it seemed, she was supposed to garrote the Nazis before they garroted her. That wasn't hard, and Sue found, to her complete lack of surprise, that she enjoyed garroting Nazis. In Round Two she was supposed to blow up a Nazi submarine — it looked a little like the sub at the end of "Raiders of the Lost Ark." Other Nazis were still chasing her, attempting to keep her from blowing up the submarine. She had to boink them over their heads with a large stick, and then plant a dynamite charge on the sub itself.

She didn't reach Round Three in the first game; a squad of Nazis caught her as she was planting the charge, shot her in the back, and then did a victory dance over her body.

Terminal Sue watched the victory dance, and found herself digging in her pocket for another quarter. Dance over her body, would they?

She made it through Round One easily, and, with some luck this time, through Round Two. In Round Three, she made her way through underground tunnels. At the beginning of the round, she'd been given a motorcycle with machine guns mounted on it. With them, she could slaughter the Nazis chasing her; every time she killed ten Nazis, she got more bullets. She was also still in possession of her stick from Round Two; any Nazis who avoided her machine guns got boinked on the head.

Midway through Round Three, bombs began dropping from the tunnel ceiling. The tunnels began crumbling around her. Terminal Sue's motorcycle tumbled into a giant gorge, and she died.

Terminal Sue said, "Damn."

With her last quarter, Terminal Sue killed Hitler, saved the free world, and put the high score on the game.

She turned her back on the game, murmured righteously, "Fucking Nazis," and went to go see what was keeping Bogie Freedom.

AFTER TELLING THE band to play something loud, something to relax the crowd, Bogie kicked the dark haired teenager out. He paused next to the doormen. "If you guys don't start checking IDs," he told them, "you're fired."

The inside doorman scratched at his cheek. "Who should check them, him or me?"

Bogie pointed at the outside doorman. "You make sure they're good looking." He pointed at the inside doorman. "You make sure they're over twenty-one."

The inside doorman said, "Right. We can do that."

The outside doorman beckoned to a cute couple. "You two. You're in."

The inside doorman checked their IDs and took their twenty dollars. Both doormen looked hopefully at Bogie.

He smiled at them. "Good job." He turned back to the club, where Bleeding Chrome was getting ready to resume its set. The lead guitarist had a couple bleeding scratches from her fight, Bogie noticed, but didn't seem to care. Probably it was a fashion thing. He headed for the back room, and then stopped dead as the Indian chick, who he'd completely forgotten, appeared in the doorway.

From twenty feet away, Terminal Sue looked straight at Bogie Freedom. Bogie stared back at her. If he could find the bouncers, he thought, he could have them throw her out.

The band started up again, something loud and relaxing.

Later, Bogie knew he had imagined it. It wouldn't be his first hallucination, nor his best. The gun simply appeared in the woman's hand. Nobody was that fast. He couldn't believe she wanted to murder him just because he wouldn't talk to her. A single shot went by his right ear so close he thought somebody had struck him on the side of the head. Then the crowd was parting around him, Bleeding Chrome joining the stunned silence.

Something made Bogie turn around.

The blond man stood motionless, still on his feet, a spreading red stain flooding down the front of a shirt even whiter than he was. Bogie stared at him in silence, watching the man as he took one step, and then another. The man lifted the gun he still held in his right hand, and pointed it at Bogie.

Terminal Sue's second shot took him in the shoulder. The man spun around, the muscles in his hand clenching reflexively.

He shot the big mirror over the bar four times.

"Oh, my God," said Bogie Freedom into the awed silence. "Do you know what that mirror *cost?* Blue Hair's *not* going to like this."

Terminal Sue halted beside Bogie. "He was going to kill you." She kept her gun pointed at the bleeding man; he was still on his feet, gun pointed at the mirror. She wondered if he was ever going to fall over and die.

Bogie couldn't take his eyes off the ruin of the mirror. "Blue Hair's probably going to fire me for this."

Terminal Sue wished the man would turn around and face them; she didn't approve of shooting people in the back. As she was considering walking around in front of him to shoot him again, the tall bartender leaned across the bar, and, with one finger, pushed the blond dude off his feet.

He toppled like a small tree, falling over at the ankles, perfectly stiff all the way down to the ground. The gun fell from his hand and bounced along the dirty tile floor to come to a stop at Bogie's feet. With one last despairing glance at the mirror, Bogie stepped over the gun. He crouched down beside the would-be murderer, touching his fingers to the man's neck. No pulse. Bogie wiped his bloody hand on his pants, and stood again. "He's dead," he announced to the waiting club.

Someone screamed.

Terminal Sue, gun still hanging from her hand, silenced them all with a stern look. "Don't think of him as dead," she instructed Bogie. "Think of him as metabolically challenged."

DETECTIVE ROCCO DENNISON said, "Let me see if I got this straight. This woman you've never seen before showed up here to talk to you, told your bartender she wanted to talk to you about Carlo van Zandt, and then killed someone she said was trying to kill you."

Bogie nodded decisively. "And broke Blue Hair's mirror."

"Wait," Rocco said. "I thought you said the victim broke the mirror."

"Well, yes," Bogie conceded. "But we're talking about ethical responsibility here."

"Ethical responsibility."

"Right. If she hadn't shot at the blond dude, he wouldn't have shot the mirror."

"But he would have shot you," Rocco said.

Bogie shook his head. "We don't know that. All we have is the word of this woman that he was trying to shoot me. He might not have been trying to shoot me. He might have been planning to shoot her. I mean, really, are we going to take the word of a murderer in something as important as this?"

Detective Dennison leaned back in his chair, wishing he'd accepted the drink the big bartender had offered him. He'd been called in by the on-scene detectives when the name of Carlo van Zandt had come up. But none of the testimony here made any sense; the only woman involved in the case at this point was the hypothetical suspect who'd plugged van Zandt.

A thought occurred to Rocco. He leaned forward. "This dark-haired woman. Did she look Indian to you? American Indian?"

Bogie Freedom stared at the detective for a long moment before answering. "No. Not really. A little like Melissa Etheridge. Or the Indigo Girls. Kinda clean cut." He said it as though he weren't quite sure what clean cut was. "Not the kind of person who hangs out at a club like this."

"You're sure."

Bogie answered without hesitation. "Positive. I've seen lots of Indians. Walkin' Talkin' Dave is an Indian, I think. And that guy who does the Keep America Beautiful commercials on TV. The one who cries."

"I think those have been off the air for a long time," said Rocco doubtfully.

Bogie nodded. "Yeah. But they were good commercials. They stay with you."

Land Sharks

BOGIE SET THE alarm and ran. He only had thirty seconds to get out of the bar and lock the door. If he didn't make it the alarm went off and disturbed the sleeping bums, the cops showed, and Blue Hair got pissed. Frankly, Bogie felt he had spent more than his fair share of time in the company of L.A.'s finest, trying to explain that dead body. And when she found out about it, Blue Hair was going to be pissed about the dead man breaking her mirror.

Not that Bogie felt the least bit responsible for *that*. So some jerk came to see him and killed someone else who had come to see him and then the dead someone else broke the mirror. It just wasn't his fault. No way.

He slammed the back door shut, locked it and checked his watch. Seventeen seconds. Not bad. He'd locked up in only fourteen seconds once, but he'd been in a rush that night.

Bogie turned east and started home. Home was six blocks away from *The Rock*, a decrepit one bedroom apartment on Highland, two blocks south of Sunset, with an attractive view of an alley.

Bogie walked rapidly, striding along. Annoyance simmered in the warm summer air around him. He'd had worse days, but not since he'd lived with Blue Hair's granddaughter Natasha. Not in at least four years, he thought. In one day his singer had failed to show up, Blue Hair's mirror was broken, and he'd had to sit with the police until four in the morning, two hours after the club was supposed to be closed. And then, in an effort to cheer himself up, after the cops and the body had all left together, he'd paused to play one last game of *Space Nazis from Hell*.

He'd played good. He always played good. No one but Walkin' Talkin' Dave could beat him, and even Dave only beat him by a little. It was killing Hitler that did it; Dave almost always managed to kill Hitler midway through Round Four, and it always took Bogie until the very end of the round.

He'd had a great game, one of his all-time best. He played like a man possessed, taking out his frustrations and anger on the game: snuffed Hitler with almost sixty seconds left in the final round, and sat waiting, watching, while all the little Nazis around Hitler shot each other to death in an orgy of violence.

He'd done *good,* he knew it. Easily a personal best, he might even have caught Dave.

And *then* –

When it came time for him to put his initials on the High Score Hall of Fame, he'd seen it.

TS: 15,205.

It was the highest score he'd ever seen on *Space Nazis From Hell.* It was at least four hundred points higher than anything Dave had ever put on, five hundred and forty points higher than Bogie's new personal best.

This was as bad as having the mirror broken.

He paused at the corner of Highland and looked back. He was being followed; his left palm itched.

The security gate at his apartment building was broken and Bogie's door was never locked. He didn't lock his door because he didn't have anything anybody would steal – and if he did, then it stood to reason that whoever stole it needed it more than he did anyway.

It took only a moment for him to slip inside. He wondered if the person following him would follow him into his home and thought that he really should lock the door.

The door opened silently while he was debating the pros and cons of locked and unlocked doors. It was the murderer from the club, the Indian woman.

Terminal Sue closed the door behind herself, locking it. "You should keep it locked."

Bogie nodded. He had almost come to that conclusion himself. "Want some wine?"

"No. I don't drink alcohol."

"Wine is what I drink at home," Bogie said. "I drink other things at other times." He went into the kitchen and opened a $4.95 bottle of chardonnay; Terminal Sue followed him. He poured a glass for himself. "Wine is a natural relaxant," he informed her. "It helps me deal with the stress of being the Entertainment Director."

"Being the Entertainment Director is stressful?"

"Yeah," said Bogie pointedly, "when your singers don't show up. And Blue Hair's mirrors get broken. Then it's *very* stressful." Terminal Sue noticed he didn't mention the man she'd killed; she wondered if he was being polite, or if the mirror and the singer really *had* caused him more stress.

Bogie, who had almost forgotten the body but was still having stress over the mirror, opened his refrigerator door, gazing doubtfully into the interior. He hated having guests. "Do you want some . . . water?"

"Do you have ice?"

Bogie opened the freezer. The ice was old and had frost hair all over it, but that was her problem. "Yes."

"Thank you," she said, "water will be fine."

Bogie filled up a glass triumphantly, and handed it to her. This was what being a successful host was all about.

"I'm sorry that man broke the mirror," Sue said, "but he was trying to kill you and I need to talk to you."

Bogie snatched her water away. "That could have been *him*," he snarled. "The one who put the new high score on *Space Nazis From Hell*. And you killed him." He glared at the murderer. "You blew it. I'm never going to talk to you, so you can just forget it. As far as you're concerned," he said bitterly, "I'm gonna be the Entertainment Director until I die."

Terminal Sue stared at him blankly. "*I* put the high score on *Space Nazis From Hell*."

Bogie examined the murderer closely. "You're lying. *You're* TS?"

"Terminal Sue," the murderer said with grave dignity. "I'm Susan Walks-Far. But you call me Terminal Sue."

Bogie stared at the woman. "TS? You're *sure*?" He started to put an arm sociably around Terminal Sue's shoulders, and then stopped – after all, she was a murderer. He picked up his bottle of wine. "Let's go sit down and have a little chat, shall we?" He smiled at the murderer, showing a mouthful of perfectly even, perfectly white teeth.

"Have your teeth been capped?" Terminal Sue asked.

Bogie quit smiling.

"WHEN WAS THE last time you saw Carlo?" Terminal Sue asked. "And what were you doing at his house the day before yesterday?"

Bogie sat perched on the portable rowing machine; Terminal Sue sat in his only chair. "You never played the game before?" he asked. "Ever?"

"Do you know anything about all these blond people?"

"You've never even *seen* the game before?"

"Was Carlo acting strange the last time you saw him?"

"Dave showed you how to beat my score, right? Jeez, and I thought I was his best friend. I can't believe he'd do this to me."

Terminal Sue took a deep breath. She thought about putting five rounds into the wall next to his head; with some people that got their attention. She had a feeling it wouldn't work with this one, though; he'd just want his glass of water back. She tried again. "You do know Carlo, don't you? He does play at *The Rock* regularly, doesn't he? He was scheduled tonight, right?"

"I can't believe you and Dave would do this to me." Bogie lunged forward. "Give me back my water."

Terminal Sue jumped up to stand on the chair and held the glass out of Bogie's reach. "I'll make you a bargain."

"Gimme back my water and get out of my apartment." Bogie thought about jumping to try and snatch the glass away, but decided hopping around like that lacked dignity. "And quit standing on my furniture."

Terminal Sue lowered her water glass and took a drink. She raised it over her head again. She felt funny, and it took her moment to realize that she was having fun. She liked standing on a cheap, fake-leather chair, holding water over her head. She was hoping Bogie would start hopping up and down, trying to get the water. Of course she wouldn't let him get it; she would hold it out of his reach forever. "You tell me everything you know about Carlo van Zandt's death, and why those men are following you, and I'll tell you how I beat Walkin' Talkin' Dave's score." She took another quick sip of the water.

"It's a deal," Bogie said. "I don't know anything about Carlo's death. Until you came and told me, I didn't know he was dead. Your turn. And I want details."

"Wait a minute," Terminal Sue said. "Carlo is dead, his house has been – forgive the phrase – trashed; and you were in that house two days ago when a bunch of blond people came by to see Carlo."

"Klaus," said Bogie. "It was just Klaus."

"And who is that?"

"Klaus Vodd. I think he's an agent. Carlo's agent, maybe."

"If he's Carlo's agent, why did you run away?"

"I didn't belong there," Bogie said reasonably.

"What were you doing there?"

Bogie's lip curled contemptuously. "I thought you said you were a detective."

Terminal Sue blinked. "I am. The best."

"I," Bogie told her, "am an Entertainment Director. Usually. And, so far as I know, Carlo is always a musician. Now, what do you think the connection is between a musician and the Entertainment Director of a club he wants to play in?"

"Do you often go to the houses of your musicians when they're not there?"

"I didn't know he wasn't there until I got there," Bogie lied craftily. "And the door was unlocked."

"Oh," Terminal Sue said.

Bogie picked up his wine glass and tossed back the dregs.

Terminal Sue sat back down in her chair. "Shit. All right," she said after a pause. "One more question."

"It's *my* turn," Bogie protested.

"Who tried to kill you tonight?"

"I dunno," said Bogie sullenly. "I doubt anyone. They were probably shooting at you and I was just standing in the way."

Terminal Sue shook her head. "Nobody's that bad a shot. I was two feet out of his line of fire or I wouldn't have gotten a shot off around you. He had his gun pointed at the back of your head. Who dislikes you enough to try killing you?"

"Everybody likes me," Bogie said with a fine disregard for the truth.

"Somebody doesn't like you," Terminal Sue said quietly. "And they followed you home."

Bogie refilled his glass, then looked up at Terminal Sue as the words penetrated. "Somebody *besides* you is following me?"

"Come here." Terminal Sue led Bogie to the window and parted the curtains slightly. "There," she said. "Across the street. The two blond guys in the Ford."

Bogie looked. Sure enough. They were parked in front of the entrance to the Protestant church across the street. "Are you sure they're following me?"

"Who else would they be following?"

"Well, you for starters. You were following me and they were following me, but, maybe, they were just following you following me."

"No," Terminal Sue corrected. "I was behind them. I followed them following you, not the other way around."

Bogie let the curtains drop and then locked the front door. He sat back down on the rowing machine and took a sip of wine.

"I don't suppose you know why they're following you?" Terminal Sue asked.

"No," Bogie said. "No idea."

There was a loud knock on the door.

Bogie and Terminal Sue stared at one another. Neither spoke.

The knock was repeated.

"It's your house," Terminal Sue whispered.

"Who is it?" Bogie called out.

A high pitched voice answered, "Land shark."

Bogie laughed. "Isn't it cool," he whispered, "the way cable keeps the classics alive?"

There was the heavy sound of flesh hitting flesh. "That's not funny," a deep voice said. The same voice continued. "Police, sir. We, uh, got a complaint about the noise."

Terminal Sue peeped out the peep hole. "It's them," she whispered.

Bogie got up and peeped out the peep hole. "What should we do?" he asked softly.

"It's your house," Terminal Sue repeated.

"Just a minute," Bogie shouted. "I'm not dressed." He looked at Terminal Sue. "Got any suggestions?"

"Well," Terminal Sue said, "if I were you, I don't think I would let them in. But, like I said, it's your house. Is there a back way out of here?"

"This is the only door." They both gazed at the door for a moment.

One of the men outside pounded on the door. "Sir? Open the door. We need to speak to you."

"Hang on," Bogie hollered. "I'm putting my pants on." He added more softly to Terminal Sue, "The bedroom window lets out into an alley."

"Sir?" The deep voice called.

Bogie and Terminal Sue ignored it.

"Shit," the higher pitched voice said. "Let's just break it down."

The door shuddered as something crashed into it.

"If you don't mind," Terminal Sue said, "I think I'll just leave through the bedroom window. Thanks for the water. You don't need to show me out."

The door shuddered again. Bogie glanced from the door to Terminal Sue's retreating back. "Hang on, I'll come with you." He grabbed the bottle of chardonnay.

In the bedroom, Terminal Sue pried the screen out of its frame. "You wouldn't like to stay and defend your home?" she asked. "Stay and fight?" She boosted herself onto the window sill and scrambled out.

"Nah," Bogie said, tumbling head first into the alley. He heard the front door crash in. "I rent." He picked himself up and pushed the screen back into place.

The lights, which had only been on in the living room and kitchen, flickered on in the rest of the apartment. "Search the place," the deep voice said.

Bogie jumped over the brick wall that formed the other side of the alley, and into the apartment complex next door; Terminal Sue followed as they hopped another fence and made their way to the sidewalk.

Out on the sidewalk, Bogie said, "Now what?"

Terminal Sue started walking north up Highland, toward Sunset. Bogie glanced back toward his apartment and fell in beside her. "I'm leaving. I suggest you call the cops. You've got two men tearing your apartment apart."

"That's it?" Bogie asked. "You get me into all this trouble, you don't bother telling me how you beat Dave's score on *Space Nazis From Hell* and now you just leave?" He paused, disgusted. "What a lowlife."

Terminal Sue smiled at him. Bogie thought it was a cold, evil smile. "*I* got you into trouble? Those guys were following you, not me. They're trashing your home, not mine. And as for telling you how I beat Dave's score, why should I? You couldn't answer any of my questions. You don't know anything about Carlo's death, you don't know much about this Klaus Vodd except that you think *maybe* he's an agent, and you don't know why you're being followed. You don't know much of anything, do you?"

Bogie said indignantly, "As a matter of fact, I *do* know a lot about Klaus. I just didn't tell you before. And don't expect me to now."

Terminal Sue turned on Bogie and took a step toward him. Bogie took a step backward, thinking that her cold and evil smile hadn't looked as bad as *this*. Terminal Sue said fiercely, "If you don't tell me everything you know, I'm going to knock you right into the street."

"Hey, hey," Bogie said quickly. "Don't get so upset. I went to a party at his house once. A long time ago, weeks and weeks. And I think he's an agent. Maybe. That's it. That's all I know about him." He offered her the bottle. "You wanna sip of this? It'll make you feel better."

Terminal Sue almost knocked the bottle out of Bogie's hand. "I don't drink, I told you that already. You went to a party at Vodd's house. I suppose, just maybe, you could tell me how to get there?"

Bogie shook his head. "No," he said. "I don't remember the name of the street. I was suffering perceptual problems that day."

"You were drunk."

Bogie tried to remember. "Maybe," he said.

"Can you take me there?"

"Will you tell me how you beat Dave's score on *Space Nazis From Hell*?"

"As soon as I find out what happened to Carlo, I'll tell you."

"Good enough. I'll take you tomorrow."

"Now," Terminal Sue said. "Take me now or I'll never tell you."

"Tell me now and then I'll take you," Bogie said.

Terminal Sue laughed. "If I tell you first you'll renege on your half of the bargain. You think I'd *trust* you?"

"I've never let you down before," Bogie said.

"We've only known one another since yesterday." Sue added resentfully, "And I've already had to kill a man for you and you weren't even grateful."

Bogie scuffed the toe of his boot on the sidewalk. "Shit," he mumbled. "You probably just like killing people."

Terminal Sue couldn't think of anything to say to that.

Bogie stuffed his hands in the pockets of his jeans and managed to look, if not grateful, at least a little guilty. "The guy lives all the way in the Valley; you really want to go now? In the middle of the night?" Bogie thought he might be sorry he ever told Terminal Sue he knew Vodd. Despite her score on *Space Nazis* Terminal Sue gave every indication of being a world class maniac.

"Yes," Terminal Sue said. "I want to go right this minute."

"Okay," Bogie sighed. "Come on. We can take my car."

THE NIGHT HAD run on too long; Terminal Sue's car was locked away in the parking structure down the street, and the sign on it informed her that she could come get it out again at 6 A.M.

"I know I've got a car around here some place," Bogie said. They had been wandering up and down the streets around Bogie's apartment for twenty minutes. It was almost five in the morning.

A car turned onto the street they were in the process of wandering up and they ducked down behind a white Camaro.

"Do you have any idea what this car *looks* like?"

Bogie peered over the hood of the Camaro. "Yeah." He pointed across the street. "It looks like that."

The car Bogie pointed to was a typical Honda, square, gray, and ugly; a bumper sticker on the back said, *Drive Like An American*. Bogie stood beside it and peered inside for a moment. "Yeah," he said, patting his pockets. "This is it, all right."

Terminal Sue looked from Bogie to the car and back to Bogie. "Are you sure this is your car? You look like you're not sure and, well, I pictured you driving something a little more . . . eccentric."

Bogie took a quick look at it over the top of his sunglasses. "It's mine," he said. He quit patting his pockets. "Someone gave it to me. I put the bumper sticker on, though." He shifted so his body was between Terminal Sue and the driver's side door handle.

Terminal Sue, watching, said calmly, "What exactly are you doing?"

"Opening the door." Bogie opened the door, slid into the driver's seat and reached across to open the passenger door. He looked at Terminal Sue. "Are you coming? I really have no desire to go see Carlo's agent alone at this time of the morning."

Terminal Sue got in. She watched Bogie reach under the dashboard and fiddle with the wires. "You're hot wiring this car."

"Yes," Bogie agreed. "I am."

"Jesus." Terminal Sue shook her head as the car roared to life. "You're stealing this car."

"No, no," Bogie said quickly. "I just lost the keys." The car jerked away from the curb and they sped down the street and through a stop sign. "I told you, it's *my* car. Someone gave it to me. You can't steal your own car." He turned left onto Sunset. "I think I'll take Sepulveda. I like watching all those bicyclists. It makes me think that, maybe, someday, I might ride a bicycle on Sepulveda and be tan and sweat a lot." Bogie paused in thought and ran a red light. "The only problem is I don't like to sweat."

"It's five A.M.," Terminal Sue pointed out. "There aren't going to be any bicyclists on Sepulveda."

Bogie shrugged. "I guess we'll take the 101 then." He floored the gas pedal, whipped the car into a U-turn and screamed down Sunset Boulevard. Cold air blew in threw Bogie's open window.

Terminal Sue, fearing the dawn, reached into a coat pocket and put her sunglasses on.

"*I* never take *my* sunglasses off," Bogie boasted. "My mother told me not to." He gestured at the wine bottle Terminal Sue now held. "Is there any left?"

Terminal Sue silently handed it to him.

Bogie killed it and threw the empty bottle out the window. It shattered in the middle of the lane. A Sliver Cloud Rolls, driven by someone drunker than Bogie, swerved to miss the breaking glass and came within inches of hitting the passenger door of the Honda.

Terminal Sue didn't think Bogie noticed.

"Roll down your window, okay?" Bogie asked. "It sticks a little."

It stuck a lot. The window jammed halfway down and Terminal Sue left it there. She wondered how Bogie knew the window stuck; there was no way this car was his. He must have stolen it before. Terminal Sue glanced at the man. Stolen the car and returned it.

They drove on through the cool night air.

"Hey."

Terminal Sue glanced at Bogie. "Yes?"

"Why are you doing this? I mean, like, Carlo wasn't – I mean, you weren't, you know –" Bogie searched for an appropriate word. "You weren't – *friends* – were you?"

"I told you. He was my client."

"Yeah, but he's dead now, right?"

"Yes. But I took his money."

Bogie was silent for a moment. "How much?"

"A thousand and twenty dollars."

Bogie slammed his hand against the steering wheel, causing the car to swerve nastily through three lanes of early morning commuter traffic. Over the chorus of honks he tried to subtract twenty-four from a thousand and twenty. "Jesus," he swore. "He paid you, um, a *lot* more than he paid me." Bogie had conveniently forgotten about the Sunday nights of slavery that should have lasted until Halloween.

"What the hell was he paying *you* for?"

"Detecting," said Bogie Freedom.

Terminal Sue's sunglasses stared at him, completely without expression, for what seemed to Bogie a very long time. He stared back, not watching the road. "It's what I do," he said, "when I'm not doing other things."

People *Were* After Him

KLAUS VODD LIVED in a small house in a nice neighborhood in Sherman Oaks. Dawn arrived simultaneously with Bogie and Terminal Sue, only dawn did it with a better attitude. It was a nice sunrise, as sunrises went. A little pink, a little blue, a streak of orange. Nice. Bogie admired it for an instant as he was parking in front of Vodd's house. "This is it." He yanked the emergency brake up.

"You're parking in front of his house?"

"Yeah."

"Can't we be" – Terminal Sue searched for a word – "a little bit slyer than this?"

"Why?"

"So if anything goes wrong," said Terminal Sue, speaking very slowly and clearly – as though, Bogie thought resentfully, to an idiot – "neighbors roused by the sound of gunshots, or screams, or whatever it is that rouses them, won't be able to tell the police about the Honda parked in front of Klaus Vodd's house."

"Oh," Bogie said. He glanced at Terminal Sue out of the corner of his eye. "You know, when I told you that I went to a party here –" He paused, waiting for a response.

Terminal Sue finally said, "Uh-huh."

"Well, I think I left a different car here. We could, like, leave in that car." He looked at her more fully to see how this was going over. "We can come get this one some other time."

Terminal Sue said, again, "Uh-huh."

Bogie traded sunglass stares with her for a moment longer. "All right, if that's how you want it." He popped the emergency brake, muttering, "Fine, *take* that attitude," ducked under the dash, stroked a pair of wires together, straightened himself, pumped gas into the engine until it screamed, and popped the clutch. The car roared half a block down the quiet suburban street, and pulled screeching to a halt. Bogie yanked the emergency brake up again. "Are you happy now?" he snapped.

"Oh," said Terminal Sue, "exquisitely."

THE CAR PARKED in Klaus Vodd's driveway was a gray BMW. Terminal Sue wrote down the license plate, 1JAS305, before going up to the front door with Bogie.

Anglos – blond Anglos – with German cars, thought Terminal Sue. Registered to a company called Fourth Kingdom Import. She glanced uneasily at Bogie, who chose that particular moment to flip his blond pony-tail back over his shoulder.

Bogie reached out a fist and rapped authoritatively on Klaus Vodd's door. No one answered. After a moment he rapped a second time. If anybody did answer the door, he was going to let Terminal Sue do the talking; and if that anybody had a gun, he was going to run away. He shot her a quick glance. She really wasn't the kind of person he liked to associate with.

"If you even *think* about saying you're a Land Shark, I'll whop you upside the head," whispered Terminal Sue.

Bogie tried to give her a reproachful look. "I wouldn't do that." But then he snickered, and Terminal Sue knew he would.

Silence. Bogie reached out a hand to the doorknob. "They must not be home."

Sue slapped his hand away. "It's not even six yet. They're asleep. Wait."

The silence continued. Terminal Sue shrugged. She had a gun. She tried the door handle, ignoring the look Bogie gave her. Locked, of course. She reached into her coat pocket for her lock picks.

Bogie reached into his coat pocket for *his* lock picks. "I can open it."

Terminal Sue snorted. "Sure."

He did it while she was snorting. She heard the gentle *click* as the door unlocked. She stared at Bogie. "Where did you learn to do that?"

Bogie shrugged. "It's easier to unlock things than to break them open," which Terminal Sue thought was undeniably true but didn't answer her question. Bogie continued, "What if there's an alarm inside?"

"Then we're in trouble."

"We're already in trouble. These people know where I work."

Terminal Sue said coolly, "*You're* already in trouble."

Bogie heard his voice getting higher and louder. "Well, I wouldn't be if it wasn't for *you*. If–"

Terminal Sue hissed, "*Hush.*" She pushed the door open and stepped through cautiously, not looking back. Bogie shut up and followed her.

There was a sunken living room off to their left, with a small desk; a lengthy, gray-carpeted corridor led away from the front door, toward the kitchen. An abundance of expensive-looking furniture filled all of the empty spaces. Bogie, having obligingly hushed, whispered, "I feel claustrophobic."

Terminal Sue didn't look at him; there were more important things to pay attention to. There was a reason she didn't work with partners – the last time she'd tried to, the fellow had ended up going into standup comedy after she fired him.

The living room was empty, and considerably cleaner than the last house they had trespassed in together. The hallway was also neat, and the kitchen was so fanatically clean it reminded Sue of her mother's kitchen. Terminal Sue could not make herself believe that anyone had ever dirtied a dish in that kitchen.

The stairway rose up from the far end of the hallway, up to the second floor. Terminal Sue glanced up the stairs, and then, mur-

muring to Bogie, "Keep an eye on the stairs," headed directly to the small desk in the living room. Bogie looked carefully at the stairs, and then at Terminal Sue's retreating back, and went into the kitchen to get something to eat. He liked the looks of the kitchen. It was clean, and it looked like there might be food in the refrigerator. He had been in houses before that had food in the refrigerator.

In the living room, Terminal Sue examined the desk. Two of the drawers were locked; she examined the locks and suppressed an urge to whistle. She didn't even recognize the make, but she doubted she could have picked either of them if she'd had all day to work. Reinforced spring-loaded steel facings covered the works. She quickly rifled the other two drawers, pausing periodically to scan items that looked promising.

JOHN BOSWORTH AWOKE with a start. There were sounds downstairs.

He was filled with an abrupt rush of rage that brought him all the way awake: that son of a bitch Schmidt was drinking his orange juice *again*.

He threw off the covers and, dressed only in his underwear, hurried down the stairs. Midway down the stairs he could see directly into the kitchen. Schmidt's head was obscured by a hat, but John knew it was him by the enormous bottle of orange juice that blocked John's view of his face. That was John's orange juice, the bottle he bought fresh every evening to drink the next morning. The only damn excuse this planet had for existing, as far as John was concerned.

In flawless German, John Bosworth yelled, "Put down that orange juice!"

Bogie dropped the orange juice. It shattered explosively on the clean tile floor.

John fled back up the stairs, back into his room, and scrambled across the bed, dragging the bedside table's top drawer open. He clutched at the revolver inside, turned and sprinted back to the stairway –

Regretfully, Terminal Sue shot him in the chest.

John Bosworth took one step forward, stopped, and then brought the revolver up, as though he intended to point it at somebody, and probably, thought Terminal Sue, he did. Bogie most likely, which was understandable, though unacceptable. She shot him again and he fell bleeding down the length of the stairs.

He tumbled the last few feet into the kitchen, and lay on the floor, staring upward, gun still in his hand, bleeding heavily, mouth moving soundlessly.

Bogie thought he had seen people do it better in the movies. He heard himself say, "You killed him."

"He would have killed you, Bogie."

"He's dressed in his underpants, Sue. He didn't even have any clothes."

Terminal Sue wondered if Bogie were in shock . . . but then, she'd heard him say stupider things even when he hadn't just seen a man get killed. "He had a *gun*," she said with what she thought was remarkable patience.

Bogie paused. "Did you get what he said?"

Terminal Sue shook her head. "It was German, I think."

Bogie looked with guilt at the body, blood and spilled juice. "Maybe it was his juice." He looked at Sue. "Did you get what we came here for?"

She shook her head. "I can't get into that desk. You give it a try, I'm going to go look upstairs."

Bogie stared at her. "We just *shot* a man. I mean, you did. We have to get out of here before somebody calls the police!"

Terminal Sue stared back blankly. "Over gunshots? Nobody ever calls the police to report gunshots. People always think it was a car backfiring." She turned away. "I'm going upstairs. Try the desk."

WERNER SCHMIDT, WHO had been sleeping soundly in the master bedroom, awoke to the sound of a car backfiring twice. Maintenance, he thought, is the key to good car care. Nobody in Los Angeles maintained their vehicles properly. He pulled on his robe and decided to go get a glass of orange juice before John woke up and started getting weird about it again. He walked out into the hallway, yawning, rubbing his eyes, and froze motionless on the landing at the top of the stairwell. Blood covered the stairs, the wall; from where he stood he could see down into the kitchen, and across the length of the hallway into the living room. His hands dropped slowly to his sides. A blond fellow with a black fedora knelt in front of Klaus's desk, working on one of the drawers. Werner turned his head ever so slightly; the kitchen floor was filthy with blood, and orange juice, and John.

Werner backed silently toward the stairs. His gun was in the holster hanging next to his bed.

BOGIE TRIED THE desk. The locks were excellent; after a good three minutes of fiddling, one of the drawers popped open. Inside were four large manila envelopes. From upstairs he heard the sound of yet another gunshot. It did not occur to him that Terminal Sue might be in trouble; he wondered briefly who she'd killed this time, scooped the envelopes into his arms, turned around and left the house, trotting hurriedly to his car.

Terminal Sue found him moments later, sitting behind the wheel of a late model Buick Regal. She slipped into the passenger seat while he fiddled under the dashboard. The engine roared to life, and Bogie Freedom pulled away from the curb, put the accelerator down on the floor and screamed off down the quiet, early morning suburb streets.

Terminal Sue said, "This isn't the car we came in."

"You killed somebody else," Bogie said accusingly.

"Well, you stole another car," Terminal Sue retorted sullenly. She didn't like this tally he seemed to be keeping. "You know, before I met you, I killed two people. Two people in my *whole life*. And they both had it coming. You have, in less than a day, managed to more than double that number."

"*I* managed?" yelled Bogie in outrage. "I didn't kill anybody. I'm just an innocent bystander to your murderous rampage."

"*All* those people wanted to kill you," she snapped. "I wouldn't have had to kill any of them if you hadn't been standing there waiting to be victimized."

"I could have ducked," Bogie said. He thought about it for a moment. "Besides, whoever it was you shot when you were upstairs, he wasn't trying to kill me."

"He would have," said Terminal Sue sullenly. "The minute he saw you. Gimme those." She snatched the envelopes off his lap, opened one and looked at the contents in a hurt silence. She'd saved the silly son of a bitch's life, and not only was he not appreciative, now he wanted to talk about the death of a man he hadn't even seen.

Finally she said, "They both had guns, and the first guy was pointing it at you. He was going to shoot you."

Bogie said in the voice he used when he was pretending to be a therapist, "Do you think, ah, *most* people are trying to kill me?" Therapists said ah and um a lot when they were dealing with paranoid serial killers with guns. They were afraid of being shot.

"Well, this guy wanted to shoot you, and the guy at the club certainly wanted to shoot you."

"Um. So you think *many* people are trying to kill me?"

Terminal Sue twitched, one hand reaching for her gun. She watched Bogie flinch with gratitude. "*Everyone* wants to kill you. If you don't shut up and drive," she said, "*I'm* going to shoot you. Shoot you dead. And then I won't have to keep killing other people to keep them from killing you."

Bogie shut up and drove, albeit a little sullenly. Pretending to be a chauffeur sucked.

WERNER SCHMIDT, BLOOD seeping out through the fingers he had clutched to his stomach, managed to depress the first button on the phone's speed dialer. The phone beeped out an Orange County number and then rang twice.

A woman's voice, tinny and faint in Werner's ear, said, "Fourth Kingdom Imports."

Werner whispered hoarsely, "Jessica?"

"Werner . . . what's wrong?"

"I've been shot. John's dead. Security's been broken. Documents taken."

"*Who?*"

"Renegades and Indians, Jessica." Werner Schmidt whispered it again: "Renegades and Indians." Then he died.

THEY SAT AT a table at Farmer's Market, in the Fairfax District, and drank black coffee, while young producers from CBS Television City, across the street, discussed their latest deals, ate yogurt and drank cappuccino.

Across the aisle from them, a 22-year old agent in an Armani suit was telling a story about how he'd cut some independent producer's throat in the last round of negotiations. Terminal Sue wanted to tell him not to make up stories. Instead she said to Bogie, "I hate Farmer's Market." She opened the envelopes, one at a time, and spread their contents across the table. "This shit's in German."

Bogie nodded wearily. "Unfortunately, not a language we speak."

Visitors

ALEC ARMSTRONG APPEARED as decrepit as his car. The car was a late '70s Buick, with good tires, bad paint, and an engine that did 0 to 60 in four and a half seconds. Bogie, too shallow to see beyond the dented exterior, wouldn't have stolen the car.

Alec Armstrong's engine was in better shape than the Buick's. He was seventy years old, gray-haired and wrinkled. His posture was good, his muscle tone excellent; he ran three miles every morning, every day of his life, and had been practicing yoga daily for almost forty years.

He parked the Buick directly in front of the "Magic" sign, checking the police report again to make sure the address was correct. Nowhere did the report mention magic. He sighed, tucked the report back in his briefcase, adjusted his tie and got out of the car.

He walked up the long stone path to the doorway. A man in, Armstrong guessed, his fifties or so, opened the door before he had a chance to knock, and said politely, "Mr. Armstrong."

Alec Armstrong didn't blink – he had, after all, seen the "Magic" sign. "Samuel Highland?"

Dreadful Sam smiled. "Call me Dreadful Sam."

"I'd like to speak to you."

"Of course." Dreadful Sam stepped back from the doorway. "Come in. I've got a fresh pot of tea brewing." He smiled at the man he knew to be a longtime CIA agent. "Chamomile. It's very good for pregnant women."

Alec Armstrong said, "I'm not pregnant."

Dreadful Sam said, "Didn't think you were."

"I'M LOOKING INTO the death of Carlo van Zandt. He lived across the street from you."

Dreadful Sam nodded and sipped at his tea. He had spoken to the police; that would be in the police report Armstrong had in his briefcase. "Across the street and down the block."

After a moment Alec Armstrong continued. "I've read the police report. I was wondering if you'd be willing to go over it again for me."

"Certainly." Dreadful Sam's calm gray eyes did not flicker. "A man and a woman came to visit Carlo, and killed him."

"How do you know they killed him? Did you actually witness the murder?"

Dreadful Sam looked at Alec Armstrong. "I watched it."

Armstrong leaned forward. "You were in the house."

"I was in my house."

"So you didn't see it."

Dreadful Sam took a sip of his tea. "I waited until he died before I went to bed."

"You didn't call the police?"

"They came by the next morning, after I woke up."

It was in the report, but Armstrong asked it anyway: "Why didn't you call them that night?"

"He was dead," said Dreadful Sam. "You understand that?"

"Yes."

"He was still going to be dead in the morning." Dreadful Sam added, "I was very tired. Sitting through a death does that to you."

"Perhaps," Armstrong said, "had you called that night, the police would have caught the murderers."

Dreadful Sam was silent a long moment. "The police," he said carefully, "aren't going to catch the killers." This was an opinion, not a prediction; Dreadful Sam was *very* careful about predicting the future. It was usually pointless, and almost always depressing. Sam continued, "These people aren't your normal average rock-and-roll-musician murderers."

"You saw them drive up?"

"Yes."

"And you knew they were murderers?"

"Yes."

"Why didn't you call the police then? Perhaps you could have prevented van Zandt's death."

"I couldn't have prevented anything." To Alec Armstrong's look of incomprehension, Dreadful Sam added, "It's not something I do." He thought to himself that Bogie probably prevented things – when he wasn't doing other things.

Armstrong sat back in his small kitchen chair, cup of tea in hand, and considered the conversation they'd been having. The man knew his name, and hadn't asked him why he was here. Hadn't asked him *anything*. He'd simply given a lunatic's answers to Armstrong's questions.

Dreadful Sam said, "I'm a magician, not a madman, Alec."

Armstrong lied swiftly. "I don't think you're mad, sir. But I do not understand your answers."

"Neither did the police."

"I'm a bit more open minded than they are."

Dreadful Sam said, "Yes."

Armstrong sighed and said, "Would you describe the murderers and their car again?"

Dreadful Sam did so, and then said, in such a way that it did not strike Alec Armstrong as even slightly melodramatic, "They're evil. Evil from the pit of Hell."

TERMINAL SUE CAME by at 1:30.

Dreadful Sam, in a gracious act, let her knock. Dreadful Sam had known Terminal Sue for . . . well, thirty years or so, regardless of how you counted it. Terminal Sue was a local; Dreadful Sam had known her parents, and his parents had known her grandparents, back in the days before the freeways had strangled Los Angeles.

Dreadful Sam was the one who had dubbed her Terminal Sue.

He had coffee brewing; Terminal Sue hated his tea. Terminal Sue and Alec Armstrong had the same police report; Terminal Sue had bribed hers out of a cop named Donnelley. Dreadful Sam wondered idly where Alec Armstrong had gotten his copy.

He ran through his story for the second time that day. Terminal Sue listened patiently, without interrupting him. She didn't understand his answers any better than Alec Armstrong had, but didn't question them either.

When he was done, she said, "I think they're Nazis."

"They're evil from the pit of Hell," Dreadful Sam said.

"*Nazi* evil from the pit of Hell."

Dreadful Sam looked doubtful. "I think they're just blond."

Terminal Sue didn't waste words. "German documents, blond people, BMWs and Mercedes Benzes; they work for a company called Fourth Kingdom Import. Reich means kingdom. They're Nazis, I tell you."

"Well, in that case, perhaps you and Bogie should try avoiding them."

Terminal Sue blinked. "Bogie? How long have you known Bogie Freedom?"

"Five years," said Dreadful Sam, "more or less. I ran into him on the beach one day. He's a good boy. Insane, but good."

"Is there anyone you *don't* know?"

Dreadful Sam said, "I get lots of visitors. I had one this morning. Alec Armstrong. I'd watch out for him if I were you."

"Is he one of the Nazis?"

"No," said Dreadful Sam. "I think he's something worse."

AT 3:46 DREADFUL Sam said, "Good afternoon, Bogie."

He hadn't let Bogie knock.

"I hate it when you do that," Bogie said. His hand was poised to rap smartly against Dreadful Sam's nose. He lowered it.

Dreadful Sam said, "Sorry," but Bogie knew it was a lie.

"It's *polite*," Bogie said, "to let people knock."

"I let someone knock this morning."

"Who?" said Bogie suspiciously.

"An old friend."

"Right."

THEY SAT AT the kitchen table and drank orange spice tea.

"I thought you were keeping an eye on him," Bogie said.

"I did. I watched the whole thing."

"But you let him get killed."

"I did what you asked me to, Bogie. If you'd asked me to *keep* him from getting killed, I'd have turned you down."

Bogie sighed. "Magicians are tricky bastards. Tell me what you saw, then."

"Is this detective work, Bogie?"

"Of course not," Bogie said quickly. "I'm just curious. He was my *friend*."

"You used to have nicer friends, then."

"No, I didn't. All my friends are scum. I have this new friend, an Indian woman – she's scum," said Bogie with conviction. "Major scum. She broke the mirror at *The Rock,* and got Blue Hair really mad. And she killed a man, too. Then she followed me home, and led this land shark to my apartment, and then forced me to drive her to the *Valley,* and then she killed a couple guys there . . ." His voice trailed off.

"Pretty bad," Dreadful Sam observed.

"She's *murderous* scum," Bogie concluded. "So Carlo wasn't so bad, by comparison." He glanced at Dreadful Sam and said casually, "So what happened to him, anyway?"

"About a quarter of five yesterday morning, a heavyset Mexican woman in a green Pinto pulled into Carlo's driveway. She went inside to see him, and about five minutes later there were gunshots. She came running out of the house, got into the Pinto, and sped away."

Bogie, to whom nothing seemed implausible, nodded thoughtfully. "Did you get a good look at the Mexican woman?"

"She was about forty, maybe fifty. Long black hair. About two hundred, two-twenty. She moved pretty good . . . like a football player." Dreadful Sam took a sip of his tea. "Had good legs for such a stout woman."

"Did you see the car's plates?"

Dreadful Sam smiled at Bogie. "California vanity plates. 2 KUL 4U."

"Too cool for you," Bogie repeated doubtfully. "On a Pinto?"

"The woman had a mole on her upper lip."

"And you could see it from across the street?"

"It was a large mole."

Bogie nodded. Dreadful Sam had never lied to him that he knew of; it did not occur to Bogie that he was starting now. "A heavyset Mexican woman, forty to fifty, long black hair, a green Pinto with plates 2 KUL 4U. And a big mole. Maybe," he said thoughtfully, "she was like, a hired gun. Maybe the blond people hired her."

"Nah." Dreadful Sam shook his head. "I think it was a lover's quarrel."

HE LET HIS last visitor knock. Twice.

When he opened the door he was dressed in walking clothes. Boots, and black jeans, and the jacket he'd been wearing the night he'd killed the girl who stood on his doorstep. The brown spot, two buttons down, was her blood. He'd washed the jacket himself, by hand; he'd taken it to the cleaners; he'd even tried cleaning it with a paste made from ground vampire's teeth, which is more expensive than you might imagine.

He'd done everything short of taking a blowtorch to it that he could think of, and in the thirty years since he'd killed the girl, the stain had never come out.

She opened her mouth to speak, and Dreadful Sam said quietly, "Claudia. It's good to see you again." To her uncomprehending look he added softly, "I thought we'd take a walk together."

Claudia

IT WAS TWO miles from Dreadful Sam's home to the beach, a walk that usually took twenty minutes. A tall man, Dreadful Sam's quick, easy stride ate the distance rapidly.

He slowed down for Claudia.

The young woman hurried along beside him; her long pale legs flickered in the lower right hand extreme of Dreadful Sam's vision. He slowed again, what had been for him a stroll became a slow saunter. When the woman's pace relaxed into a good steady walk, Dreadful Sam said, "It is Claudia, isn't it?"

"Yes, how did you know?"

Dreadful Sam said, "Magic."

Claudia nodded. "Of course."

The magician examined her. She looked good. Nothing like he remembered; thirty years ago she'd been deathly beautiful. Now she was just an attractive young woman, radiating health and confidence. Dreadful Sam thought that he might like her better this way. "You look good. Better than you did when I killed you."

Claudia just looked at him. "I'm not dead."

"No."

"So when did you kill me?"

"More than three decades ago, now."

They walked on for more than a block. Elsewhere in the country you could buy an entire town for what some of the houses they passed by cost. Dreadful Sam didn't look at the houses. He didn't look at the glowing green landscapes, the blood-red roses, dappled with sunlight and groomed to perfection, or the pretty blue Westec Security signs that sat posted in every other front yard. He didn't look at Claudia. He watched the frozen black cement unwind beneath his feet.

Claudia said into the silence broken only by the sound of the passing cars, "How could you have killed me over three decades ago? I wasn't around then. I'm barely thirty."

"You couldn't be, could you?" Dreadful Sam observed. He had always known she would come back to him, but he'd rather expected it to be an act of revenge. This Claudia seemed to him curiously innocent. She didn't even know him.

He could follow her thoughts without trying, without looking at her, as the woman tried to decide how seriously to take him. "How come you killed me?"

"You were bad." He still didn't look at her. "And I loved you."

The worst thing was, she didn't even know him.

THE WALK TOOK forever. It took Dreadful Sam and the woman he'd already killed once forty-five minutes to reach the Pacific Ocean. Before they'd covered a mile of the two mile walk, Sam knew that he didn't want to know Claudia again.

She had been bad before, and she was bad now.

Some things never change.

"Do you know something about the murder that happened the other night?" The wind caught a strand of dark blond hair, casting it up and across her face. Dreadful Sam wanted to reach out and push it away. He wanted to touch her and he wanted very much not to touch her.

"I know all about it," said Dreadful Sam. "I watched it happen."

"You were in the house?"

"I was in my house." Dreadful Sam smiled at her. "You haven't seen the police report."

"Should I have?"

Dreadful Sam shrugged. "Everyone else seems to have a copy. You should try to get one. It can't be hard."

"Who killed Carlo van Zandt?"

Dreadful Sam smiled at her again. "You did. And you're about to ask me about Bogie Freedom."

It stopped Claudia as she was opening her mouth. That had been her next question. "You do know him, then."

Dreadful Sam stopped walking. He stood there on the pavement with the cars zooming by at fifty and sixty miles an hour, staring at Claudia. "Bogie's a good boy. I'd take it poorly if anything happened to him."

Claudia Hess shivered visibly. Something about the way the man said it. She didn't want to know what "taking it poorly" consisted of, not when he had just told her that he'd already murdered her once.

"When did you meet him?"

"Five years ago," said Dreadful Sam. "More or less."

THEY MADE LOVE on the beach, in the darkness, with the sound of the waves in Dreadful Sam's ears.

Afterward he thought grimly, dreadfully, *I'll have to kill her soon.*

CLAUDIA PUSHED HER way into Klaus Vodd's office, in the industrial park in Irvine where they were renting space. She didn't knock.

Klaus Vodd looked at her with blatant irritation. Sitting across from him was an elegant looking man in an expensive suit. "Claudia," said Klaus. "This is our good friend, Michael Grant."

A touch surprised, Claudia looked at the man more closely. She had expected a skinhead – a "redneck," the word was. This fellow looked as though he'd just come from a Chamber of Commerce meeting, not as if he were the leader of the neo-Nazi movement in Fontana, California.

Grant stood as Claudia entered, stood there with his hand outstretched. "Miss Hess. A great pleasure." He spoke with an accent that was an odd mixture of Los Angelean and Southern cracker. It reminded Claudia of home, that mixture of accents . . . though to be sure, the people at home tended to mix German and English, not Los Angeles and Alabama.

Claudia took his hand. "Mr. Grant, I've heard good things about you."

The man smiled at her, showing capped teeth against a tan that Claudia suspected came from a tanning parlor. It was perfectly even, contrasting with his pale blue eyes, and it struck Claudia that he was actually rather handsome. The thought left her cold; she compared him in her mind to the wizard, and shivered.

"I've heard good things of you, also," Michael Grant said politely. He paused. "Did you know you have sand in your hair?"

"Yes."

Vodd interrupted. "If you could excuse us, Claudia. We have some business to conclude. I'll see you when we're done."

Claudia's eyes narrowed. She didn't like being dismissed – but there was no point in fighting in front of the help. "I'll be in back."

She went into the back storage area, brushed the sand out of her hair and washed her face. She heard them out front, raised voices at one point; she heard the front door open and headed back down the hall to Klaus's office.

She ran into the good looking Fontana Klanner in the hallway. "Excuse me. I thought I heard you leave."

"Just went out to my car to get some papers," said Grant. He held the door to Klaus's office open, and Claudia shrugged and headed back inside with him.

"I thought your second in command should hear this," Grant said to Klaus as Claudia seated herself on the small sofa facing them both. Grant tossed a sheaf of papers on Klaus's desktop. "This is the report my people compiled on that asshole van Zandt. The man's from fucking *Topeka.*" The contempt in his voice was unmistakable. "You know that? Of course you don't know that. None of you know how to run a goddamn TRW report, do you?"

Claudia wondered who the hell this guy thought he was. "Not a lot of use for them, where we come from," she said. "No credit cards. On the other hand, we do know how to blow fucking Fontana off the map. Hydrogen fusion, Mikey boy." She smiled at him. "Got kids, don't you, Mr. Grant? Couple of little sheet-wearing Klanbabies?"

The man paled beneath his tan. It was an interesting sight. "You threatening me?"

Claudia laughed at him. "Yeah. You know the difference between us and you, Grant? If we decide to blow someone up, we don't have to work with alarm clocks for detonators. Wouldn't *you* like some toys like that?"

Klaus interrupted. "That's *enough.* From both of you. We don't need squabbles among people devoted to the Cause."

"Why didn't you just run this guy's fingerprints?" Grant demanded. "You shot him on what, a guess? You *hoped* you were right?"

"The operative in question," said Klaus, "destroyed his file before leaving. We don't have his fingerprints. We don't have any information on him except what people remember about him, and he wasn't a sociable fellow. We haven't seen him in close to six years, and we're working with reproductions of an eight-year old photo we found in his mother's effects." He slid open a drawer, reached inside it, and snorted in disgust as Michael Grant tensed visibly. "Relax," he said dryly. "If we wanted to shoot you, we'd have done it before now." He took a flat manila envelope from the desk, extracted a photo from it and flipped it over to Grant's side of the desk. "This is Adolph Stiegler."

Grant picked up the photo. It showed a thin young man with blond hair and eyes that might have been blue, in a slightly fuzzy photo. "Adolph, huh?"

Klaus said, "We know the Renegade has had contact with that club, *The Rock*." Klaus shrugged. "And the Renegade plays the guitar."

Just from the photo, it might have been half the young neo-Nazis Grant had ever met in his life. The fellow in that photo *could* have been Carlo van Zandt . . . or Bogie Freedom, for that matter. Michael Grant wouldn't have minded killing Bogie Freedom, if only because of the name. "Well, I see the resemblance. But you jumped the gun, you should pardon the expression, on this van Zandt fellow; you shoot every blond guitarist in L.A. and you're going to wipe out a quarter of the city." He shrugged. "Not that *that* wouldn't be a good idea. Now . . . this Freedom fellow . . . there you might have something. He doesn't have a driver's license. He doesn't show up on TRW reports. He does have a tax record, but it only dates back four and a half years."

Claudia and Klaus exchanged a glance. Klaus said, "Sounds like it could be our guy."

Grant stood up. "I'll leave the report with you. The next time you decide to kill somebody, check first, all right? I'd hate to see the lot of you in federal custody the next time I turn on the television set. I *do* want some of those toys you promised me." He paused, added smoothly, "Soon," and left.

When he was gone, Claudia said flatly, "That magician, I talked to him for quite a while."

Klaus was looking over the papers Grant had left; without looking up he murmured, "In the sand?"

Claudia said, "He knows we killed Carlo, and he knows we're interested in the Freedom guy. He's a dangerous man."

He did look at her now. "You're overreacting, Claudia. How could he know something like that?"

"He's a magician," Claudia said slowly, as though explaining to someone who should know better. "And he kept talking about killing me as though it were something he'd already *done*. I think maybe it was a threat."

Klaus looked at her with disbelieving exasperation. Claudia was one of the best operatives he'd ever seen; but she had a mind of her own, and it went off in thoroughly odd directions at times. "That's an odd thing to be unsure about."

Claudia leaned forward on the couch. "We need to take care of this situation, Klaus, and get the hell out of here."

"Kill Freedom, then."

Goose bumps touched the back of Claudia's neck. She didn't want to try and kill Bogie Freedom; the magician would take it poorly. "We're not sure it's him," she said.

Klaus looked as though he were holding on to his temper. "We weren't sure it was Carlo, either. We know our guy is connected with that club. Freedom is the only other one who fits the description. You *kill* that bastard Freedom," he repeated.

Claudia Hess was afraid to kill Bogie. She thought that if she killed Bogie, Dreadful Sam would kill her.

Again.

Pie Heaven

THERE WAS A message on Terminal Sue's answering machine when she got to the office Tuesday morning.

It was from Bogie.

"Look, we can forget about Klaus. Those guys you killed, they weren't involved. It was a Mexican woman who killed Carlo. I'll tell you more about it later." There was a long pause, and Terminal Sue thought the message had ended, and then Bogie said, "Please don't kill anyone else, okay?"

Terminal Sue snorted in disgust. It wasn't like she killed somebody every day. She glanced at her watch: 8:20 A.M. She hadn't killed anybody in over twenty-four hours.

She ran a magnet over the message tape to wipe it clean, and made a note to herself to tell that idiot Bogie not to leave messages on her machine that accused her of killing people.

Before she left she read both the *Los Angeles Times* and the *Daily News* to see if there was any mention of murders in Sherman Oaks. None.

The Nazis had cleaned up after her.

THE BOUNCER DIDN'T check her ID, didn't question her right to go in, and didn't make her give him ten dollars. Bogie glanced up from *Space Nazis From Hell,* then glanced back down again quickly. "You," he snarled, and left it at that.

Terminal Sue had heard nicer greetings. "Come on. I wanted to take you for a ride."

Bogie didn't look up. "To where?"

"To see our translator, first. And then to go visit a mutual friend."

"We don't have any mutual friends," Bogie said. "We only just met."

Terminal Sue watched Bogie struggle through his last man, the motorcycle zooming through the crumbling subterranean tunnels, and then accept defeat as the Nazis machine-gunned Bogie's last man and danced upon his quivering corpse. Terminal Sue gazed thoughtfully at the machine, and then said, "These blond people are Nazis."

Now he looked up from the game. "You've been playing too much *Space Nazis*. It's a video game, you murderer. It's not real. I told you, a heavyset Mexican woman killed Carlo."

"That's why you need to go see the translator, Bogie. And our mutual friend. It wasn't a heavyset Mexican woman who killed Carlo. I'm telling you, Bogie. These guys are bad and they're blond."

Bogie resisted an urge to touch his ponytail and glared at her. "You know, not all blond people are Nazis. Not all blond people are even German." He finished triumphantly. "Not even all German people are Nazis."

"I never said –"

"I knew this guy once, he was blond *and* from Germany *and* named Fritz, but not even he was a Nazi."

"These people are."

"Nah." Bogie shook his head. "I don't think so."

"Fourth Kingdom."

Bogie didn't know what fourth kingdom was supposed to mean, but his unfortunate train of thought went: fourth kingdom, heavenly kingdom, seventh heaven – fourth heaven, that would be . . . "Pie heaven?"

Terminal Sue shook her head in disgust. "It's the company their cars are registered to. Reich means kingdom, Bogie. Hitler's was the third Reich, the third kingdom; and these people are running a company called Fourth Kingdom."

WITH THE TOP down and the music blasting, they roared east along Sunset Boulevard, through stretches that looked like something out of Tijuana, and on toward downtown. Bogie leaned back in the passenger seat of Sue's Mustang and basked in the mid-morning sun. "This isn't so bad," he said. "Make sure you don't get me in any shade. Don't drive near any tall trucks."

Terminal Sue nodded. She pumped the volume on the stereo and inundated Bogie with Melissa Etheridge.

Bogie watched her from beneath his sunglasses, surreptitiously, as she drove. He tried not to smile; it would just make her suspicious. The chick had looked like Melissa Etheridge, he'd told the cop. Or the Indigo Girls. And now here she was, playing Melissa.

Over the music Terminal Sue said, "You know, our translator was very offended by the contents of the documents I gave her."

Bogie winced. He wished she would stop saying *our translator*. It made it sound as though he were involved in this mess. "She's *not* my translator. I don't have any translators. I've got bartenders, bouncers, waitresses. No translators."

Terminal Sue glanced at him. "You owe me a hundred and seventy five dollars for half the translating fee."

"These papers better say something good. What's in them?"

"Nazis. According to the documents, they're working with a group out in Fontana –"

"There's Nazis in Fontana," Bogie conceded. "I saw this episode on *Hard Copy* –"

"You watch *Hard Copy*?"

Bogie thought about it. "Maybe it was *A Current Affair*. Anyway, they had a big story about how Fontana was the Neo-Nazi capitol of Southern California."

They sped inland, eventually arriving in Koreatown. Sue made a quick left hand turn, darting across the left hand traffic and coming to a stop in the shabby parking lot of a tiny corner mall. Sue didn't put the top up.

Bogie glanced at her cellular phone and her two thousand dollar stereo. If he was a thief, he thought, conveniently forgetting that he was, he would steal them.

Terminal Sue said, "Nobody in Koreatown steals things from my car. They know me here."

Bogie, who was not from Koreatown, thought that he would steal the whole car. He looked out at the mini-mall doubtfully. "Our German translator works in a Koreatown mini-market?"

"No." Terminal Sue got out of the car. "She works above the mini-market."

Bogie trailed after Terminal Sue, through the grungy parking lot, through the equally grungy mini-market, and then through a door that led to a rickety, unpainted stairway. Bogie stopped and examined the stairway. During the last earthquake he had seen a stairway that had cracked completely in half. This one *had* cracks in it, big ones, and Bogie looked at them doubtfully. He waited until Terminal Sue was halfway up the stairs before following her. If the stairway cracked in half, he thought, he might leap off in time to save himself. Terminal Sue had demonstrated that she could take care of herself.

There were two doors at the top of the stairs, a red one and a green one. Terminal Sue hesitated, and then knocked firmly on the green one. Bogie released a sigh of relief.

The door opened to the extent permitted by the door chain, and an elderly Korean woman peered out. She said something incomprehensible.

Terminal Sue said, "Is Juliet home?"

From the rear of the apartment Bogie heard a voice call out. "Sue? Is that you? I'll be right there," followed by a burst of what

Bogie assumed was Korean. The old lady unchained the door, beaming at Terminal Sue and favoring Bogie with a suspicious look, and then led them inside, to the back room.

The room contained a narrow bed, a desk, and a single straight-backed chair. Terminal Sue sat down on the bed and gestured to Bogie to sit next to her. He did, gingerly. The bed squeaked loudly. Terminal Sue turned to glance at Bogie. He tried hard not to blush.

A young Korean woman burst into the room and dropped into the single chair. "Sorry. I was in the bathroom." She dug into one of the drawers of the desk and came out with the papers Bogie had liberated the day before, along with a neatly typed sheaf of paper. "This stuff's disgusting, Sue. Where did you find it, anyway?"

"In the Valley," Terminal Sue said. Terminal Sue gestured at Bogie. "Julie, Bogie Freedom. Bogie, this is Juliet Wu. You owe her a hundred and seventy-five dollars."

Juliet Wu looked at Bogie. "*You're* Bogie Freedom?"

Bogie wanted to deny it. "Yeah. You heard of me?"

"Man, your name is all over these papers. These guys hate you. You and Carlo van Zandt. It says in one of the papers here, a report to their superiors I think, that they were going to kill Carlo, and then they were going to kill you too."

"See?" Terminal Sue said triumphantly. "Everybody does too want to kill you!"

"Nazis," Bogie said. "Only Nazis want to kill me."

Juliet Wu looked at him expectantly.

Bogie looked back at her.

Finally she said, "Do you want to know *why* they want to kill you?"

"I *know* why they want to kill me," Bogie said despairingly. "God, I never should have done it. Fuck Blue Hair, anyway."

Juliet said to Terminal Sue, "What's he talking about?"

Terminal Sue said, "Why do they want to kill him, Juliet?"

"He's a deserter," Juliet said gleefully. "A Nazi deserter. A *blond-haired* Nazi deserter."

"Huh?" Bogie said. "You mean it's not –"

"Not what?" Sue asked.

"None of your business," Bogie snapped.

"You're a Nazi?" Terminal Sue asked. She mimicked him: "'I knew this guy once, he was blond *and* from Germany *and* named Fritz, but not even he was a Nazi.'"

"*I'm* from Santa Barbara," Bogie snapped. "People from Santa Barbara don't become Nazis. They become Republicans."

"You're a Republican?" Terminal Sue asked.

"That's almost as bad," said Juliet. She eyed him suspiciously. "Are you gay?"

"No."

"Do you smoke?"

"Yes," said Bogie, before he realized she meant cigarettes.

Juliet nodded thoughtfully. "A white heterosexual Republican male supporting the tobacco industry." She looked at Terminal Sue. "He could be."

"Could be what?" Bogie asked.

"Almost anything," said Juliet.

OUT IN THE parking lot, walking toward the car, Bogie was almost speechless with rage. "You," he began.

"Get in the car," said Terminal Sue.

"She," Bogie began.

"You see those clean white people sitting in the BMW down the road?" Terminal Sue asked. Bogie started to turn his head, and Sue jerked on his arm. "Eyes *front*," she snapped. "They don't belong here."

Out of the corner of his eye, Bogie could see them; two men and a woman in a white BMW. The woman sat behind the wheel. "Don't tell me," Bogie sneered. "They're white Republican Nazis."

"I don't know what *they* are," said Sue. As they approached the Mustang, she said, for the pure joy of saying it, "*You're* a white Republican Nazi." When Bogie opened his mouth to reply, she added, "Get in the car or I'll leave you here."

The rear-view mirror was angled perfectly; Bogie, in the passenger's seat, could see the BMW parked on the opposite side of the street. "Did they follow us here?" he asked.

"I didn't see them on the way in, and I was looking . . . but I hope so." Terminal Sue's severe features looked even grimmer than usual. "Otherwise they know where Juliet lives. And they know that she had their documents." She hit the ignition, and let the engine idle for a second. "Bogie?"

"Yeah?"

"Don't scream, okay?"

SHE BURNED RUBBER in the parking lot and hit the street doing forty miles an hour. By the time she had reached the light at the corner she was doing sixty and Bogie had his seat belt on. She whipped the Mustang right, onto Sunset, and glanced over at Bogie to see if she was scaring him.

He had leaned his seat back to catch the sun.

For the first time since meeting Bogie Freedom, Terminal Sue almost liked him.

She took the onramp onto the 101 freeway at ninety. In her rearview mirror she could see the BMW, well back. At 11:45 on a Wednesday the traffic was just loose enough to enable her to weave in and out through the gaps in the commuter traffic. The BMW followed her down onto the freeway ... bad news, maybe. The BMW was faster than her Mustang. But Sue was confident of her ability to outdrive them. She was a Los Angeles native and *nobody* knew the freeways better than her. She had it worked out in her mind, and she could do it: take the 101 to the 110 south, take the 110 south to the 10 east, the 10 east led to the northbound 5, and then zoom up the northbound 5, which would feed them into the 101 northbound, which would take her back to Sunset Boulevard, which would take her to Dreadful Sam's house. Avoid the police, avoid the other traffic, lose the Nazis, protect the paint job because her insurance rates were high enough to *begin* with –

All while keeping Bogie in the sun.

"I can do that," Terminal Sue announced, whipping them over onto the ramp leading to the 110 south.

"Hey, hey," Bogie said, never opening his eyes.

"Underpass," Terminal Sue said apologetically. "Unavoidable." With one hand she punched Juliet's phone number into the cellular phone. The phone rang once and Juliet picked up.

"Hello?"

"This is Sue," Terminal Sue yelled in the direction of the phone. "Someone was waiting for me outside your apartment. Is there someplace you and the old woman can go, spend a couple nights?"

"A couple nights? Sure. Is that all it's going to take?"

Terminal Sue said, "Yes," and hung up.

They flew down the 110 freeway through the lunch time crowd. Terminal Sue considered dropping off the freeway onto one of the side streets. She dismissed the 2nd street off ramp instantly; the tunnel would keep them out of the sun too long. The 4th street off ramp would drop them into Echo Park, where Sue was sure she could lose their pursuit; she knew the back streets in Echo Park extremely well. But there were pedestrians there; Terminal Sue had learned a long time ago that it was a bad idea to have car chases around pedestrians.

She decided to make it as simple as possible. The white BMW was visible far back in her rear-view mirror, but they had gained slightly since her last glance. If she kept this up for any length of time they might actually catch her, which would be embarrassing. She pulled the Mustang over into the far left hand lane –

And slowed down.

The BMW came zooming up behind her, weaving in and out of traffic at high speed. Terminal Sue admired the driving; it was good, almost as good as hers, clearly the work of someone who was enjoying herself. Sue waited until the BMW was within five car lengths of her Mustang, and then hit the accelerator and spun the wheel. They skated across five lanes of traffic, barely missing a semi, into the 10 west onramp. The Nazis, blocked by the truck, were trapped in traffic in the far left lane of the 110 south.

Terminal Sue waved to them.

Bogie said, "Underpass?"

Terminal Sue replied, "Truck."

Evil From The Depths Of Hell

TERMINAL SUE PULLED the Mustang into Dreadful Sam's driveway and parked it next to the big sign that said "Magic."

Bogie Freedom opened his eyes. "Hey," he said. "This is where Dreadful Sam lives."

Terminal Sue said, "Yes. I know."

"Damn," Bogie said morosely. "I was hoping we didn't really have any mutual friends."

THE SMELL OF spaghetti permeated the house.

The table was set with three plates.

"You lied to me," Bogie said accusingly.

"For your own good," Dreadful Sam replied soothingly. "And I made you spaghetti."

"Is there human hair in it?" Bogie asked.

"Should there be?" Dreadful Sam asked. "There might be orange cat hair in it, but it would probably blend into the sauce." A big orange tom allowed Dreadful Sam to feed him on occasion.

"If this is some kind of magical shit," Terminal Sue said, "I don't want to hear about it."

Dreadful Sam wasn't surprised by the comment; Susan was less comfortable with magic than practically anybody he'd ever met. If he hadn't known both of her parents, he'd have wondered at times if she was really an Indian. Dreadful Sam knew any number of Indians; he was a quarter Cherokee himself. Magic didn't bother most of them. "It's not magic," Dreadful Sam said. "At least the cat hair isn't." He added, "You can do a lot of interesting things with human hair, though."

"It wasn't a stout Mexican woman," Bogie said. "It was Nazis."

"I don't think you should associate with Nazis, Bogie. I think they'd be a bad influence on you." Dreadful Sam glanced at Sue.

"But then again, I think Susan's probably a bad influence on you, too." He tried to imagine somebody being a good influence on Bogie, and couldn't.

"2 KUL 4U," Bogie sneered. "You think I wouldn't have figured this out as soon as I tracked down that license plate?"

"Do you know *how* to track down a license plate?" Terminal Sue asked.

"I could figure it out."

Dreadful Sam smiled. It was one of the things he liked best about Bogie; Bogie probably could have figured it out. He ladled pasta out onto the three plates. Terminal Sue poured wine into a pair of glasses while Bogie sat at the kitchen table. Bogie watched her resentfully; she knew where things were in Dreadful Sam's kitchen. Obviously she'd been there before. Lots. "How long have you two known one another?"

Dreadful Sam paused a good long time before answering. "Twenty-nine years," he said finally, "close enough. I saw Susan the day she was born. After she killed a man when she was fourteen I gave her her nickname, the name she had when I met her."

"He had it coming," said Sue swiftly. She had often thought that that nickname had warped her entire life; sometimes she resented Dreadful Sam for having given it to her.

Dreadful Sam shrugged. "Until you killed that fellow, I wasn't sure it was you."

Bogie's lower lip thrust out slightly. No one had known Bogie his entire life, and he didn't like the fact that Dreadful Sam had known Sue *her* entire life. It struck him abruptly that Terminal Sue had probably known *lots* of people her entire life. Aside from the people Bogie had known before his mother died, none of whom he had any desire to see again, not in this life, the only people he'd known for any length of time were those at *The Rock*. And Dreadful Sam.

Dreadful Sam poured sauce over Bogie's pasta. "You want some cheese, Bogie?"

"I'm not hungry," said Bogie sullenly.

Terminal Sue put down the wine glasses, one for Dreadful Sam and one for Bogie, and sat down. "Here. Do Nazis drink Chianti?"

Bogie glared at her. "I drink tea when I'm here. I drink rum and pineapple juice when I'm the Entertainment Director, and I drink whiskey when I'm detecting. I never *ever* drink red wine."

"Except when you're being a priest," Dreadful Sam said.

"Oh, yeah." Bogie shrugged and picked up the glass Terminal Sue had handed him. "Hail Mary." He drank half of it.

"He's a Nazi," Terminal Sue told Dreadful Sam. "That's why the Nazis want to kill him. He's an operative who deserted."

Dreadful Sam peered over the rim of his wine glass at Bogie. Bogie had been any number of things. He could be a Nazi, Dreadful Sam supposed, when he wasn't being something else . . . but it didn't feel right. Dreadful Sam shook his head. "Nah. Bogie's from Santa Barbara. He told me so."

"He was probably lying," said Terminal Sue. "He's a liar."

"*Dreadful Sam's* a liar," Bogie said. "'Moved well for such a stout woman,'" he quoted.

"I am a liar," said Dreadful Sam. "When I feel like it. But I am very hard to lie *to*."

"What's that got to do with anything?" Bogie demanded. "*I* never lied to *you*."

"I think that's what he just said," said Terminal Sue. "He doesn't think you lied to him. *He* thinks you're from Santa Barbara." Her tone of voice indicated what she thought of that. She dug into her spaghetti.

They ate spaghetti in silence for several minutes.

"I really think the two of you should give this up," Dreadful Sam said. "I don't think you want to mess with these people. Bogie, you go to San Diego for a little while. When you come back, everything will be fine."

"And what's Terminal Sue going to be doing while I'm in San Diego?"

"She's going to be in Nevada," said Dreadful Sam. "She's got people in Nevada."

"I do?" Terminal Sue asked, surprised.

Dreadful Sam nodded. "Aunts, uncles, cousins."

"You've been talking to my mother again," Sue accused.

"No." Dreadful Sam shook his head. "I've met these people. I've been to Nevada. I ate dinner with your Aunt Elise."

Terminal Sue had never heard the name before. "Well, I'm not eating with her," Terminal Sue said. "Because I'm not going to Nevada."

"And I'm not going to San Diego," Bogie chimed in.

"If she wants to eat with me," Terminal Sue said, "she can come to L.A."

"Look at me." Dreadful Sam gathered them both in with his eyes. He had known Susan Walks-Far her entire life, and he loved her. She had cried in his arms after she killed the man who'd had it coming. And Bogie . . . Bogie, for whatever incomprehensible reasons, had found a place in his heart. He wanted the boy to visit, wanted to listen to him talk. He liked to hear the way Bogie thought. "The people you're facing aren't human." Dreadful Sam, who knew the devil, knew about people who weren't human. He had no wish for these two friends to know what he knew. "They aren't normal."

"I'll say," Terminal Sue murmured.

Bogie, who Dreadful Sam liked to hear talk, kept silent.

"They're evil from the depths of Hell." Dreadful Sam sighed. They weren't listening to him, didn't understand. Couldn't understand. "From a place of brimstone and molten lava," he added softly. If they died, it would break his heart; and it would change everything.

"DROP ME OFF at *The Rock*," Bogie said as they pulled out of Dreadful Sam's driveway. It was almost three o'clock, and he had to be to work at four.

"I don't think you should go back there," said Sue. "These guys who want to kill you, they know where you work. They know where you live."

"Yeah," Bogie said. "But if I go there, Blue Hair gives me money."

"Which you can't spend if you're dead," Terminal Sue pointed out.

Bogie shook his head stubbornly. "I got a deal with her. Between four and two-thirty A.M. I'm the Entertainment Director. She expects me. Besides, nobody wants to kill Entertainment Directors." He looked at her pointedly. "Just detectives. Lots of people want to kill detectives."

Terminal Sue didn't look at him. She tried to think the way he thought. She wanted to say something he would understand. "Maybe," she said, "the Nazis don't understand that you're the Entertainment Director between four and two. Maybe they think you're always a detective." She shook her head. "I don't think Nazis have a lot of entertainment."

Bogie looked at his watch. "If you don't drive me," he said, "I'm going to take a bus. I have time."

Terminal Sue knew he wouldn't take the bus; he would just steal a car. She pointed the car in the direction of *The Rock*. Perhaps, she thought, if she simply stayed at *The Rock*, she could just kill all the

Nazis who came to kill Bogie. She frowned. The death toll was getting out of control. That cop, the one who wasn't as dumb as his flatfoot Irish partner, he was going to start noticing if people kept dying around Bogie.

Tawdry Sex

THE TALL BARTENDER looked at her when she walked in the door. "Hey, Chief."

Terminal Sue smiled at him. It wasn't a nice smile. "You Indian?"

The bartender frowned. "I'm a bartender."

"What's your name?"

Bogie, on his way toward the back, said over his shoulder, "That's Dave. Walkin' Talkin' Dave Bradden." He stopped and grinned at Walkin' Talkin' Dave. It wasn't a nice grin. "Hey, Dave. This is the chick who beat your score on *Space Nazis*." He turned around and went into the back room.

Walkin' Talkin' Dave and Terminal Sue eyed one another warily. Walkin' Talkin' Dave said finally, "Good score."

"Thanks."

"You want a drink? On the house?"

"Mr. Bradden." It was an old, *old* voice. Terminal Sue turned. The woman was a hundred if she was a day. She had eyes like chips of ice hidden away in the folds of her face, a nose that hooked out and down and a chin that hooked straight up. She was dressed entirely in black, with a pink and white cameo at her throat.

She looked like a witch and her hair was blue.

"How, Mr. Bradden, will we make money if you give our liquor away? Charge the young lady." The old woman moved off gracefully, barely using the black walking stick she carried.

When she was far enough away that Terminal Sue didn't think she could be overheard, she said, "Does she need that stick?"

"Not to walk with."

"So, it's like, a threat?"

"Uh-huh."

Terminal Sue nodded. It was a pretty good threat for an old lady.

Dave leaned over the bar, smiling. "You want to hear something cool?"

She shrugged. "Sure."

"Every year since I've worked here, four years in a row, we've celebrated Blue Hair's hundredth birthday." His eyes gleamed with delight, with the certainty that he'd told her something that she'd enjoy just as much as he did.

Terminal Sue looked at him blankly. "Then she's a hundred and four."

"No, no. She's a hundred. She's a hundred *every time*. Isn't that great?"

"It's impossible."

"Of course it is," said Dave impatiently. "Isn't it great, though?"

"It's crazy," said Terminal Sue. "Talking to you is as bad as talking to Bogie."

Dave said warily, "You're going to ruin this, aren't you?"

"MR. FREEDOM."

Bogie refused to look away from the game. "Yeah?"

"You broke the mirror."

Bogie lost a man. The Nazis did a victory dance over his body. He looked up sullenly. "It wasn't my fault. It was the Indian chick. She shot the guy who shot the mirror."

The old woman examined him. "We're talking about ethical responsibility here, Mr. Freedom." Bogie hated that phrase. "If you hadn't foolishly allowed this man to try and kill you, the 'Indian chick,' as you put it, wouldn't have been obliged to shoot him. Carelessness, Mr. Freedom. Pure carelessness, I say. You are responsible for the security of this establishment. You hire the bouncers. You train them. They should not have let murderers *into* my club, is that clear?"

"I'm going to hire Bubba," said Bogie quickly. "From *UnClean Joe's*. Nobody gets by Bubba."

Blue Hair took another step toward Bogie, obliging Bogie to take a step backward. He didn't want to get within range of the stick. "I won't tolerate this, Mr. Freedom. No more broken mirrors. No more murderers getting past the door. If the 'Indian chick' is required to shoot any more of my patrons, I will be most displeased. The mirror cost eight hundred and thirty-two dollars to replace, Mr. Freedom. Eight hundred and thirty-two dollars. And nineteen cents. I will begin deducting it at eighty-three dollars and twenty-two cents per paycheck, from your paycheck." She'd rounded up, Bogie noted resentfully.

She made her slow and stately way back to the office.

Bogie went out into the front. "Hey, Dave," he said, "lend me a hundred and seventy-five dollars."

Dave pulled a wad out of his pants pocket. He peeled two hundred dollar bills off and handed them to Bogie. Bogie turned around and handed them to Sue.

Terminal Sue looked at the bills suspiciously. "What's this for?"

"The translator," said Bogie. "Now you owe –" He did the math quickly. "Four hundred and sixteen dollars and ... ten cents," he said. "For the mirror. And I want twenty-five dollars change."

IN THE PARKING lot, she said to him, "How old is Blue Hair?"

"A hundred."

"She's not a hundred and four?"

"Of course not," said Bogie.

"And how old was she last year?" Terminal Sue asked carefully.

Bogie hesitated, and Terminal Sue suspected that he knew. "Well," Bogie hedged, "if she's a hundred this year, she must have been ninety-nine last year."

Terminal Sue nodded. All right. As long as they all knew that Blue Hair wasn't *really* a hundred every year, Terminal Sue could live with it.

THE CLUB STARTED to get busy around 9:30. Terminal Sue stayed in back and played *Space Nazis*. Before the evening was over she had filled the top ten list on the game's High Score table, wiping out the WTDs and BFs. Now it said TS, ten times. Bogie should like *that*.

When the ruckus started, she hurried out into the front, afraid somebody was murdering Bogie. No one was murdering Bogie; it was just a fight between half a dozen long-haired musicians. Terminal Sue watched as one guy tried to shove his drum sticks up another musician's nose. She gave him points on technique; he got it in almost three inches.

Bogie and two bouncers waded in and broke it up. Bogie backhanded one of the musicians, kneed one of the others in the stomach, and grabbed a small one by the scruff of his neck. The crowd watched with a degree of admiration; they appeared to understand that they were watching a *great* Head Bouncer at work.

Bogie Freedom might not be much of a killer, Terminal Sue thought, but he understood crowd control.

Terminal Sue watched the crowd watching Bogie, and wondered if she was going to have to kill one of them.

"HEY, CHIEF."

The band was taking a break. Terminal Sue sat at the far end of the bar, watching the room. The other two bartenders were taking care of the drinks that needed to be made; Walkin' Talkin' Dave stood on the other side of the counter, looking at her.

Terminal Sue looked back, examining him curiously. Not a bad looking man, even if he did keep calling her 'chief.' "Are you trying to piss me off?"

He grinned. "If I was trying, I would have done it already."

Terminal Sue nodded. Probably true. He seemed like a talented fellow. "Don't call me 'chief,'" she instructed him. "Call me Terminal Sue."

He smiled at her. "You can call me Dave."

Terminal Sue glanced away, keeping an eye on the older blond people in the crowd. There were a lot of blondes, but most of them were younger than the Nazis she'd run into. The Nazis she'd seen so far were mostly in their thirties and forties; she doubted there were three or four blond people in the room tonight that old. Not looking at Walkin' Talkin' Dave, she said, "Where you from?"

"Los Angeles," he said, "born and raised. County USC is still trying to get my Dad to pay for me."

"Really?" She glanced back at him, looked him over a little more closely. "Any Indian blood?"

"Some," said Walkin' Talkin' Dave. "But I don't know exactly what. My mother had some, but she didn't talk about it. How did you meet Bogie?"

"We have mutual enemies," said Sue. "You live around here?"

"Not too far away."

Terminal Sue nodded. "What are you doing tonight?"

Walkin' Talkin' Dave grinned at her. His teeth were startlingly white. "No plans."

Terminal Sue nodded again. "Want to take Bogie home with you?"

DOCTOR DEATH AND Kathy showed up at 10:30.

Bogie Freedom had known them both almost as long as he'd been in Los Angeles. He suspected that they were sisters, but he'd never gotten around to asking. They looked alike: blond women with blue eyes, almost radiantly healthy. Doctor Death, a vegetarian, was a waitress at one of the finest steak houses in L.A.; Bogie ate there sometimes. Bogie didn't know what Kathy did; she seemed to be habitually unemployed.

They came to *The Rock* a lot.

They took up positions at one of the tables near the door, and Bogie made his way over to say hello. He stopped at the table and paused to admire them before saying anything.

Doctor Death said, "Broke Blue Hair's mirror, huh?"

Kathy *tsk*ed and said, "Must have cost a lot to get it replaced."

Bogie said, "How do you know about the mirror? Neither of you have been in since then."

"Oh, it's the talk of the town," Kathy assured him.

"You're becoming a public figure," Doctor Death observed. "We just came over to look at you tonight."

"We don't know many public figures," said Kathy.

"Nate, over at *UnClean Joe's*, he said he was going to get your job after Blue Hair fires you."

"Blue Hair would never hire Nate in a million years," said Bogie sharply.

"So she *is* firing you," Kathy said.

"I'll quit first," Bogie snapped.

"Well, you can't come work at my restaurant," Doctor Death said. "You'd bring the undesirables around."

Kathy didn't say anything. Bogie knew she didn't have a job to protect.

"WHO ARE THOSE blond women talking to Bogie?" Terminal Sue asked Walkin' Talkin' Dave.

Walkin' Talkin' Dave peered through the gloom. "That's Doctor Death," he said. "And Kathy. They come in all the time."

"Doctor Death," Terminal Sue said. "What the hell kind of name is Doctor Death?"

"An appropriate one," said Walkin' Talkin' Dave.

BOGIE SCOWLED AS Terminal Sue approached their table. "This is the murderer I was telling you about," he told Doctor Death and Kathy. "The one who's ethically responsible for the broken mirror."

"No," Kathy corrected him. "*You're* ethically responsible for the broken mirror. You run the club."

"I didn't break any mirror," Terminal Sue told them. "I just shot some guy. It was to save Bogie's life." She faced Doctor Death. "Walkin' Talkin' Dave says you're Doctor Death."

Doctor Death nodded. "Doctor Death, MD. They don't let me practice anymore."

Terminal Sue looked at the woman. She looked . . . *nice*. She looked like the sort of girl Bogie would want to take home to his mother, if Nazis had mothers. She wore a little too much leather, but she had a clear schoolgirl complexion and big schoolgirl eyes. Sue wished Doctor Death would put her sunglasses back on; they hung by one ear piece from the front of her white silk blouse.

Doctor Death smiled at her and Sue winced. She didn't look like death. "How many people have you killed?"

Doctor Death said, "Only the ones who needed it."

It was a good answer; Terminal Sue smiled, a bit reluctantly. "The ones who *asked* for it, right?"

"Practically begged for it. I'm a pacifist at heart."

Terminal Sue blinked. "I wouldn't go that far. Sometimes violence is the best solution . . . and sometimes it's just fun." She turned to Bogie. "What are you doing tonight?"

"Working," Bogie said shortly.

"After work. I don't think you should go back to your apartment."

Bogie looked at Doctor Death. Doctor Death looked at Kathy. Kathy looked up at Terminal Sue. "We'll take him home with us."

BACK AT THE bar, Terminal Sue said to Walkin' Talkin' Dave, "You're off the hook. Doctor Death and Kathy are taking Bogie home."

Walkin' Talkin' Dave looked envious. Doctor Death and Kathy shared *everything*. "What are you doing tonight?" he asked Terminal Sue.

"Working," she said shortly. "I promised a friend I'd take care of this problem by Thursday."

"*This* problem?"

"The Nazis," said Terminal Sue. Walkin' Talkin' Dave simply nodded, and Terminal Sue felt gratified. She'd assumed Bogie had told the man everything, and obviously he had. Bogie Freedom was a walking security risk. "But it's just temporary," she assured Dave. "I'm taking care of it."

"How about," said Walkin' Talkin' Dave, "you go take care of it in the morning? And we do something else tonight?"

"SHE'S TREACHEROUS," BOGIE Freedom said at 2:44 A.M., kissing Doctor Death's breast. He'd felt weirdly betrayed when Terminal Sue had gone off with Walkin' Talkin' Dave. He didn't want Walkin' Talkin' Dave to like Sue better than he liked Bogie. Dreadful Sam *already* liked Sue better and had known her longer.

"A treacherous, no-good, low-down, disaffiliated, mechanically aptituded gun-stroking Indian," Bogie continued. He shifted over, kissing Kathy's breast, the nipple hardening as his tongue danced against it. He didn't want her to feel left out. "But that's okay," he said. "I'll deal with her in the morning."

Dreadful Sam

CLAUDIA SAT ON the pier at Santa Monica, her pantyhose tucked into the shoes that sat beside her. There was a cool wind off the ocean and she closed her eyes and leaned into it, blouse unbuttoned to the third button, letting herself drift as the wind touched her in intimate places.

Outnumbered though they were, unable to trust anyone but themselves, there were advantages to this work:

Claudia found that she loved the sea.

She went to the beach during the day when she was able. It was not as often as she'd have liked, but that was unavoidable. There was work to do. Sometimes, though, as she watched the sun set across the Pacific, watched the tide crawl in and out across the densely packed sand, watched the sun rise cold and gray over the misty beaches, Claudia understood why the Renegade had abandoned them.

He'd probably been a poor choice from the first. He had a sense of humor and more than a touch of cynicism. Claudia had known him as well as anyone else, and better than most, though that wasn't saying much. Adolph had generally stayed to himself, and particularly so after his mother's death. He was a talented man, though; good with languages, good with machinery, not afraid to be by himself during the trip. Claudia had envied him the opportunity to go –

And now that she was here, she knew that she had been right to envy him. The sea was *such* an amazing experience. The sight and smell and feel of it against her skin. The second mission had already been planned when Adolph set out; Adolph had known that Claudia was going to be following him within a few years. They'd talked about it together; going to see the ocean was one of Adolph's secret goals. He'd confessed it to her, before they sent him out –

She almost couldn't blame him. It wouldn't stop her from killing him, though. Adolph's disappearance had slowed that second mission by almost two years, and increased its size by a good bit, to ten.

Two of them, Klaus and Gunther, were security officers; they couldn't afford to let this one fail.

Not if they wanted to survive.

NOT LONG AFTER midnight she walked north along the beach front.

She'd been certain he would be there.

He was.

He sat in shadows on a jumble of rocks near where they'd made love two nights ago. He blended into the blackness; black walking boots, black jeans, a black long-sleeved shirt. She couldn't quite see his face and for a long eerie moment, looking at him, he looked like the shell of a man, just the outline, as though something had eaten him away from the inside.

Her voice caught. "Sam?"

He stood up and moved toward her, and the illusion persisted; his face was in shadows and there was no face where his face should have been. Terror touched her, flooded into her, the fear she had briefly conjured for herself, the fear she had imagined when the magician had talked about killing her, and she moved backward, stumbling –

He stepped into the light from the street lamps. In the harsh glare he was only a handsome man, a little older than she usually liked. "I was waiting for you," he said.

Her pulse thudded in her ears. "You scared me."

"I'll do worse than that," said Dreadful Sam, "if you keep coming back."

Claudia didn't doubt him. She had never encountered anything like the wizard, not at home, not since she'd been here. When he talked of magic, she believed that magic was real. When he spoke of the devil, she caught the taste of something so black and so cold it made her want to take up religion.

There was a power in him, and a doom, and they called to her.

She whispered, "Take me home with you."

IN THE HOUR before dawn, they lay together, side by side, not touching one another. They lay naked in the warm summer air, covers thrown aside, sweat cooling on them; Claudia on her side, looking at Dreadful Sam, Dreadful Sam on his back, hands clasped behind his head, staring up into eternity.

A single candle, on the headboard above the bed, illuminated the room dimly. The candle flickered despite the lack of a breeze.

"Bogie Freedom," said Claudia finally, "is one of us."

Dreadful Sam did not look at her. "No. No, he's not."

"He came to Los Angeles five years ago," Claudia persisted. "There are no records of him prior to that point. He's ours, Sam."

Dreadful Sam said in a deep, passionless voice, "No." Claudia imagined that it was what a granite statue would sound like, if it spoke. "The man you want to kill is a blue-eyed bastard like the rest of you."

That much was true; the Renegade was blond with blue eyes, like Claudia, like Klaus; like most of them. "You're telling me Freedom doesn't have blue eyes?"

"Green," Dreadful Sam whispered. "They're green, beneath those sunglasses." He rolled over, pinned her beneath him, and spread her legs with his.

Claudia Hess said in a slow, distracted voice, "I won't be fooled by contact lenses."

Dreadful Sam entered her, and before he lost his train of thought entirely, said, "I'll show you tomorrow."

What The World Is Coming To

BOGIE PULLED UP outside Dreadful Sam's house in a car that did not belong to him. Dreadful Sam had called him at Doctor Death's apartment and requested that he come over. How Dreadful Sam had known to call him there was a question that never crossed Bogie's mind. Magicians had their ways.

On the other hand, the simple fact of the call made him vaguely uneasy. As far as Bogie knew, Dreadful Sam didn't call people. Bogie hadn't even known that Dreadful Sam had a phone. Had a black crow appeared on Doctor Death's windowsill, croaking out, "Go to Dreadful Sam's, go to Dreadful Sam's," Bogie would have been much happier with the situation.

Dreadful Sam was waiting for him. He sat on the porch in front of the house, in the late morning sunlight, reading the L.A. Times. He shook his head as Bogie approached. "Dodgers lost again," he said.

"Republicans control the town," Bogie replied.

Neither of them said, *What is the world coming to.*

"What did you want me for?"

"I want you to meet someone," said Dreadful Sam. He folded up the newspaper and stood up. "We're going to go meet her at the plaque of James Dean, in Griffith Park."

The answer astounded Bogie. "You're going to . . . get in a car?" he asked. "And go someplace?"

Dreadful Sam stared at him with pale gray eyes. "Yes."

Bogie shook his head. "No, no," he said. "That's not right. You never go anywhere."

"Sure I do," said Dreadful Sam dryly. "I just do it behind your back."

Bogie said it. "What is the world coming to?"

IN THE 1969 Mustang that Bogie had acquired that morning, they drove toward the Hollywood hills.

"This is a nice car," Dreadful Sam commented.

"I plan on putting it back where I found it," Bogie said.

Dreadful Sam nodded. "People notice when cars like this disappear."

Bogie turned left at Western and drove north, turned right at the jog in the road. "I like the way this car handles," Bogie said. "You know, in *The Rocketeer* –"

"The what?"

"It was a movie," said Bogie. "*The Rocketeer*. About this guy who gets a jet pack and becomes a superhero. I always wanted a jet pack," he said wistfully.

Dreadful Sam turned to look at him. "What about it?"

"There were Nazis in that movie," said Bogie. "And they had a shoot-out at Griffith Park. The hero got away with his jet pack."

"Yeah," Dreadful Sam said. "Well, they also shot that scene in *Rebel Without a Cause* there, the one where James Dean and the other guy race up to the edge of the cliff, and the other guy goes over the edge and dies."

Bogie nodded. "That was a good movie." Neither of them spoke after that. Several minutes later Bogie pulled into the parking lot at the observatory. At noon on Wednesday, about forty cars were parked at the observatory, come to see the laser light show set to the music of Pink Floyd. Two school buses were parked in the end of the lot farthest from the observatory. A crowd of children milled around outside the ticket booth.

A blond woman that Bogie had seen before, the one who had chased them in the BMW, stood next to the plaque of James Dean, on the other side of the park. Bogie pointed at her. "That's one of the Nazis," said Bogie. He didn't open the door or make any motion toward getting out of the car.

Dreadful Sam said, "Don't point."

"Terminal Sue said these people want to kill me," said Bogie doubtfully. "You brought me to meet people who want to kill me?" He couldn't bring himself to distrust Dreadful Sam, although everything indicated that he ought to.

"They don't want to kill you," said Dreadful Sam. He knew it for a fact. "They want to kill someone else. Once they know you're not their guy, they'll leave you alone."

"How do I prove I'm not their guy?"

"Take off your sunglasses," said Dreadful Sam. "The guy they want to kill has blue eyes. Yours are green."

Bogie shook his head. He didn't take off his sunglasses or his hat. Well, he took his hat off when he bathed. "I'm not taking them off. Not for any damn Nazis."

"Do you want them to kill you?"

Bogie looked at Dreadful Sam sullenly. "No."

"Then you have to take off your sunglasses."

"How do *you* know I have green eyes?"

Dreadful Sam snorted and didn't bother to answer him. Instead he got out of the car and started across the lot, not waiting to see if Bogie followed.

Bogie let him get halfway across the parking lot, before reluctantly easing his way out of the car. He stood beside the car, watching Dreadful Sam approach the blond woman. When he was close enough, the woman reached out her hand and laid her fingertips against Dreadful Sam's sleeve.

Bogie got back in the car and started the engine. The wizard could take care of himself, nobody was going to kill Dreadful Sam . .

. but somebody might kill Bogie. *Bogie* hadn't sold his soul to the devil: nobody was looking out for Bogie except Bogie, and it suddenly struck Bogie that he had to start doing a better job of it.

Bogie backed the red Mustang out of its spot, narrowly missing a dude on a motorcycle who had just come zooming into the lot behind him. Bogie hit the gas pedal, moving much too rapidly in the lot, zooming down the row of cars toward the exit.

Dreadful Sam turned away from Claudia and sprinted, moving far faster than a man in his late fifties should have been able to. He darted out into the narrow road that led away from the observatory, jumping directly into the Mustang's path.

He stood his ground as the Mustang came rushing toward him.

Bogie, who would have run a Nazi down, couldn't run Dreadful Sam down. He slammed on his brakes. The car fishtailed, spinning, and the rear bumper brushed Dreadful Sam's pant leg. Dreadful Sam stepped around the car, yanked the driver's door open, and hauled Bogie out of the car by his shirt front.

"I told you," Dreadful Sam said furiously, "that you'd be safe. What in Satan's name do you think you're doing?"

Bogie, who had never seen the magician angry, couldn't respond. It was a thoroughly impressive sight.

"I promised these people a look at you," Dreadful Sam continued, still angry, "and I didn't do it for *their* sake, I did it to keep *you* alive!"

Somebody slugged Bogie high on the shoulder.

Bogie stumbled back away from Dreadful Sam, turning to see who had slugged him.

The man on the motorcycle, the man Bogie had almost run over, stood on the hood of a Honda fifty yards away, both hands clasped around a black automatic, pointing it at Bogie.

He fired again. Bogie heard the shot this time, heard the windows in the driver's side door shatter.

Dreadful Sam, who had ceased to terrify Bogie, shoved him into the open door of the car, actually kicking him to get him over into the passenger seat. Bogie's nose smashed against the window on the passenger side. It hurt. Dreadful Sam scrambled in after him, behind the wheel of the still running car, the door slamming shut behind him. They faced into the parking lot, toward Claudia, toward the man who was still shooting at them from the top of the Honda. A bullet hit the windshield. Safety glass burst upon them in a storm of small fragments.

Dreadful Sam got the car into reverse and floored it. They roared backward out of the parking lot, backward into the street leading away from Griffith Park, hitting forty miles an hour without slowing.

Dreadful Sam's last view of the park was of Claudia, running toward them, shooting at him.

He got out into the street, out of the line of fire, and spun the wheel. The car slewed around at high speed, almost flipping over, and Dreadful Sam got it pointed in the correct direction, heading south, back down into the flatlands, roaring past the Greek Theatre at high speed.

The Nazi on the motorcycle came after them. Dreadful Sam saw him in the rear view mirror, coming up fast. The man got within twenty feet of the car, gun in one hand. A bullet shattered the rear window, spraying Dreadful Sam from behind with safety glass –

Dreadful Sam stomped on the brake. The motorcycle ran up on the car's rear end, tossing the Nazi up onto the trunk. The man rolled off the trunk as the Mustang came to a halt, landing in the street.

Dreadful Sam, because he was already going to Hell anyway, put the car in reverse and ran over both the man and the motorcycle, and then drove away at a sedate pace.

Dreadful Sam glanced over at Bogie. Bogie sat almost erect, deathly pale, one hand pressed against the wound in his shoulder, trying to staunch the bleeding. Blood trickled down his face. Dreadful Sam said, "You're not going to be able to return this car."

Bogie, who didn't want to think about the blood pulsing from between his fingers, down his chest, and pooling in his lap, said, "We need to get rid of it. We're never going to be able to clean it up, and the police are going to be able to trace it to us."

Dreadful Sam nodded. The boy was thinking clearly. "You're taking this well," he observed.

Bogie said, "My face hurts."

When the safety glass shattered it had hit Bogie in the face, giving him half a dozen shallow cuts that were barely bleeding. His face hurt, Dreadful Sam thought. Not his chest, not his arm; his face hurt. Christ. "We need to get to a hospital."

"Jesus, I'm bleeding, I can't believe how much I'm bleeding. *Stop!*" Bogie yelled abruptly.

Dreadful Sam slammed on the brakes. The car screeched to a halt at the intersection of Western and Sunset Boulevard. "What? *What is it?*"

Bogie stared at him. "I saw a phone."

"A phone?"

"I have to call Blue Hair and tell her I'll be late."

Answers

TERMINAL SUE MET Dreadful Sam in the lobby of the hospital. "How is he?"

Dreadful Sam said dryly. "They dug the bullet out of him half an hour ago. They gave him a local anesthetic, and the entire time they were digging the bullet out of him he kept worrying that Blue Hair was going to fire him."

Terminal Sue nodded. She understood his fear; she'd met Blue Hair. "Who shot him?"

"A mugger," said Dreadful Sam.

"A blond mugger?"

"Quite."

Terminal Sue nodded. "You take care of him. I'm going to go take care of *them*."

"Could you take care of something else for me, first? There's a trashed red Mustang parked illegally outside emergency. Could you make it disappear?"

"You have the keys?"

Dreadful Sam tried to remember if there had been any. "No. I don't think Bogie –"

Terminal Sue said, "Got it."

ROCCO DENNISON SAID to the man in the hospital bed, "You understand it's a crime to lie to the police?"

"Are you calling me a liar?"

Lying there in the hospital bed, Bogie Freedom was wearing his sunglasses. He had asked Dreadful Sam to go look for his hat; he hadn't been able to find it since being wheeled out of ICU, and now he had hat hair.

He would be able to lie to the cops better, he thought, if only he had his hat.

"Not yet. What were you doing at Griffith Park?" Rocco asked.

Dreadful Sam, sitting in the chair next to the hospital bed, said, "We went to go see the laser show."

"Pink Floyd," Bogie said helpfully.

"The Wall," said Dreadful Sam. *"Good* Floyd, from before Waters left."

"And you got mugged by a motorcyclist and a blonde lady," said Rocco, referring to his notes.

"Right," said Bogie, nodding vigorously.

"And then you ran over the motorcyclist with your Mustang."

"No, no," Dreadful Sam said. "It was a Toyota. A red Toyota."

Bogie glanced at the magician, nodded, and said sincerely, "Red."

"How do you two know each other?" Rocco asked.

"I'm his father," said Dreadful Sam.

Bogie glanced at Dreadful Sam, neither denying nor confirming the statement. He knew Dreadful Sam was lying; Bogie's mother had neither known nor cared who Bogie's father was, but he hadn't been Dreadful Sam.

Rocco examined them both. They didn't look anything like each other. "You're lying."

Dreadful Sam smiled. "Only in the most literal sense."

Rocco shook his head. You couldn't trust anything these damn magicians told you. "You tell fortunes," he said.

"I tell people what's going to happen to them, sometimes," Dreadful Sam clarified. It wasn't the same thing. "Would you like to know what's going to happen to you?"

Detective Rocco Dennison shivered visibly under the magician's pale gray eyes. "No. I don't want my fortune told. I want to know how you two are involved in Carlo van Zandt's death. I want to know how you're involved in the death of a man we still haven't identified, over at *The Rock* on Sunday night. I want to know who the woman was who shot the man at *The Rock*. *I want to know what caused this goddamn mayhem in the streets today!*" By the time he got done, he was yelling, red-faced.

Bogie looked impressed.

Dreadful Sam looked annoyed. He said, "You're going to die three days before your fiftieth birthday. Do you want to know how?"

Bogie had always thought that the phrase "the blood drained from his face" was just something that happened in stories. Now, beneath the hospital's fluorescent lighting, he watched it happen. Rocco's florid red features went white in the space of two or three seconds. "I'm forty-eight," he got out finally.

Dreadful Sam sat back in his chair and nodded. "Stop yelling at Bogie," he said wearily.

"They were muggers," said Bogie helpfully. "We were driving a red Toyota. Maybe they thought we were rich."

"Good Toyotas are expensive," added Dreadful Sam. "Ours was top of the line." It was true enough; Dreadful Sam had a client who owned a red Toyota Supra, and who owed Dreadful Sam many favors. It was a thirty thousand dollar car. Dreadful Sam regretted the necessity, but he saw no way around it; that Toyota was going to have to turn up somewhere, shot up and banged up. Ideally it should have Bogie's blood inside it, but that wasn't going to be possible; the boy had already lost enough of his blood.

Dreadful Sam missed the days when you could fool the cops by matching blood types – Dreadful Sam didn't even know if there *was* any magic that would fool DNA tests.

From the hallway, Bogie heard a soft, cold voice murmur the words, "Entertainment Director."

"You can check on our story," said Bogie helpfully. "The car's out in the lot. It's the one with the windows shot out."

Dreadful Sam had to keep himself from wincing. Detective Dennison finally looked away from Dreadful Sam long enough to give Bogie a long look. "Check on it," he said at last. "I'll do that. I'll be right back."

After he was gone, Dreadful Sam said to Bogie, "A word of advice."

"Yes?"

"When talking to cops, don't use the word 'story.'"

"I did it on purpose," Bogie said. "I'm hoping he finds out I'm lying, and comes back and shoots me to death."

The door Rocco had just left through opened. Blue Hair stood in the doorway.

Bogie wished desperately for his hat.

"Mr. Freedom," said Blue Hair softly. "You are not at work."

TERMINAL SUE, WHO had called her oldest younger brother from the hospital, had him park her Mustang on the street outside her house. She parked Bogie's borrowed Mustang herself, in the garage. Her brother had offered to drive Bogie's Mustang – and Sue knew he could have hot-wired it, probably faster than she could – but if police stopped them on the way home, she didn't want her brother driving a car with the windows shot out, and the passenger seat covered with Bogie Freedom's blood. Terminal Sue *knew* cops; they would view such a situation suspiciously.

Sue lived in a Spanish architecture collection of bungalows, three blocks north of Sunset, within walking distance of her office. The garage was her only real luxury; it was large enough for three cars at once. She parked the stolen Mustang in the space where she usually kept *her* Mustang, and pulled the Jag out from the space next to it, to give Rodrigo space to work. She parked the Jag on the street.

Rodrigo was twenty-four years old, and had yet to hold an honest job. He'd have the car in parts by midnight. He slipped in under the garage door as Terminal Sue pulled it down.

"Can I sell the pieces?" he asked. "Or do I just have to get rid of them?"

Terminal Sue examined the car doubtfully. "Don't sell anything that has a bullet hole in it or blood on it."

"Cool," Rodrigo nodded. "That still leaves me a lot of car." He eyed his sister thoughtfully. "We could go into business, you know?"

Terminal Sue shook her head. "I have a business. I'm –"

" – the best private detective in Los Angeles, yeah, yeah."

Terminal Sue thought sometimes that having family was more trouble than it was worth. You never got any respect from them, no matter how amazingly good you were.

"Mom says you should come visit her," Rodrigo added. "She says you're ungrateful."

"Start cutting," said Sue.

"I'M BLEEDING," BOGIE said quickly. "Wanna see?"

Blue Hair shook her head. "What I want, Mr. Freedom, is for things to return to normal. I am tired of having my mirrors shot. I am tired of having my Entertainment Directors shot. I am tired of having my singers fail to show up because *they've* been shot. I rather expect my Bar Manager to be shot at any moment, and in all, Mr. Freedom, I am of the opinion that entirely too many things have been shot of late. You seem to be running with what, in my youth, they called a 'gun crowd.'"

Bogie nodded; Terminal Sue made up a gun crowd all by herself.

Rocco Dennison burst back through the door. "There's no goddamn car outside," he said. "The emergency nurse said some Mexican woman came and stole it."

"Was she stout?" Bogie asked.

Dreadful Sam laughed out loud.

"Is this funny to you?" Rocco Dennison demanded.

"Well, parts of it," said Bogie.

Blue Hair peered at the Detective with narrowed black eyes. "You are?" she asked.

"Detective Rocco Dennison, LAPD."

"The police." She smiled, and Rocco took a step backward. "What are you doing to look into these unfortunate shootings, Detective?"

"I'm trying to get information from these guys," said Dennison.

Blue Hair glanced at Bogie, who tried to look innocent. She nodded as though every suspicion she'd ever had of him had just been confirmed, and turned back to Dennison. "Do you often interrogate victims of crimes in their hospital beds, Detective?" Blue Hair was certain that Bogie was guilty of something, but she wasn't going to let somebody else push him around. If Bogie had done something wrong, *she* would see that he suffered for it. "Mr. Freedom and Mister –" She paused.

"Dreadful Sam," said Dreadful Sam. He smiled at her quite pleasantly. She smiled back, quite pleasantly. The sight astonished Bogie.

"Mr. Freedom and Mr. Sam," Blue Hair continued, "were set upon in a public place by hooligans. Perhaps you should go back to your police station, dig up some of your mug shots, and bring them back so that the victims of this terrible crime can identify their attackers. That strikes me as a sensible path."

It was more or less what Rocco had intended to do next anyway, but after being commanded to do so by this ancient woman, he didn't want to any more.

"And you should try to find our stolen Toyota," Bogie said.

"The license plate," said Dreadful Sam, "is 2 KUL 4U."

A panicked look flashed across Bogie's face, vanished.

Rocco addressed Blue Hair. "They're involved," he said, "and I'm going to –"

They never did find out what Rocco was going to do. A doctor shouldered her way into the increasingly crowded room. "Mr. Freedom," said the doctor. "I'm Doctor Badoui." Doctor Badoui was a short, stout woman with a dark complexion. Interestingly, except for the fact that she did not have a mole, she looked very much like the mental image Bogie had of the woman who Dreadful Sam had claimed had killed Carlo van Zandt. She had good legs. "The rest of you are going to have to leave," she said, "while I examine Mr. Freedom."

Blue Hair said, "No."

"Okay," the doctor said. "You can stay. You two have to leave, though."

Dreadful Sam said, "No."

The doctor glared at Rocco. "Get out!"

Rocco said, "But –"

Doctor Badoui yelled, "Security!"

Rocco fled.

Doctor Badoui yanked Bogie into a sitting position.

He yelled and slapped her hands away. She dropped him and he slammed back against the wall behind him. "Ouch!"

"Good reflexes," said Doctor Badoui. "Any dizziness?"

Red spots danced in front of Bogie's eyes. He lied. "No."

She examined the chart. "One gunshot wound, superficial cuts. You're going to have bruises and scars, Mr. Freedom . . . are you having difficulty with the light, Mr. Freedom?"

Bogie looked at her from behind his sunglasses. "No. The light is fine."

Doctor Badoui said mildly, "You might see things a touch better without your sunglasses, Mr. Freedom. You might even find it a bit easier to drive at night." She hung the chart back at the foot of Bogie's bed.

"How long will it be until Mr. Freedom can return to work?" Blue Hair demanded.

"He should stay in bed for at least two days," the doctor said. "And then take it easy for another week or so."

Blue Hair said to Bogie, "I will expect you at the club once you are discharged from the hospital, Mr. Freedom."

Bogie glared at her. "She just *said* I should take it easy for a week."

Blue Hair murmured, "That will be quite in keeping with your usual job performance, then."

LATE THAT EVENING, as visiting hours drew to a close, Dreadful Sam got up to leave.

Bogie said, "Dreadful Sam?"

"Yeah."

"You shouldn't have told that cop that the license plate on the Toyota was 2 KUL 4U. He'll look it up."

Dreadful Sam shook his head. "A red Toyota Supra that belongs to a friend of mine will turn up over on La Brea tomorrow morning. It'll be shot up the way that Mustang was. It's a real car."

Bogie stared at him. "You really know somebody whose car's plates are 2 KUL 4U?"

"I know all sorts."

Bogie thought about it for a moment. "Dreadful Sam?"

"Yes?"

"That cop, Dennison . . . is he really going to die three days before his fiftieth birthday?"

Dreadful Sam stood there in the hospital door, and then nodded *yes*, and a hard shiver ran down Bogie's frame.

Dreadful Sam said gently, "Good night, Bogie."

TERMINAL SUE PARKED her Mustang on a side street two blocks away from the industrial park that was listed as the business address for Fourth Kingdom Import. She had a fully loaded Blackhawk tucked in a holster inside her coat, a hideaway .38 tucked into her belt at the small of her back, and spare clips for both in her coat pocket.

She didn't intend to take any attitude from any Nazis.

She checked the directory at the front of the business park. Fourth Kingdom Import was located at Space 19. Space 19 was a big warehouse, with a dead-bolted front door. A security light glowed above the doorway.

It was nearly midnight. The park was empty, quiet except for the sounds of distant traffic.

Terminal Sue knocked on the front door. She heard a shuffle of movement from inside, and took two steps to the right, out of the line of fire.

A voice said from the other side of the door, "Yeah?"

Terminal Sue hollered back, "Security. Your alarm's going off, buddy."

"No it's not."

"The silent alarm," Terminal Sue said. "It's the silent alarm. You must have triggered it. I gotta turn the damn thing off or the cops are gonna be here in the five minutes. Then I gotta fill out reports all night, and you gotta put up with cops trooping through your offices."

She stopped and waited.

After considerable unlocking, the door was pulled open. Light spilled out onto the walkway, intolerably bright in the midnight gloom. A thin young man, about twenty-five, peered out through the opening. Terminal Sue grabbed his shirt front, yanked him out through the door, and put her gun up under his chin. "Shhh," she said politely. "Anyone else inside?"

"You're not security," he whispered.

"And you didn't answer my question," she replied.

"There's a couple other guys," the young man said quickly. "Three."

"Good," Terminal Sue said. "Then I don't need you. I can shoot you now."

"I'm alone."

Terminal Sue pushed him back in through the door, following him into a brightly lit front office. She stood just inside the doorway, waiting for her eyes to adjust, ready to shoot anything that moved.

Nothing moved.

The young man stood motionless, staring at her with obvious fear . . . and something else. "You're the Indian," he said.

"I'm Terminal Sue," said Terminal Sue. "At least get the name right. Who are you?"

"Andrew Peak," he said. "Where's the Renegade?"

The corner of Terminal Sue's mouth twitched. The no-good Republican Nazi renegade was trapped in a hospital bed where he couldn't get into any trouble, couldn't get up to any of his no-good Republican Nazi renegade tricks. Santa Barbara my ass, she thought.

Sue suppressed the smile. "Wrong approach. You don't ask me questions, *I* ask *you* questions. I've got the gun, and a friend of mine is lying in the hospital right now leaking blood from holes you people put in him. I'm in a very, *very* bad mood." They stood in a hallway outside a row of offices; Terminal Sue gestured to the pipes exposed along the warehouse walls. "You kneel over there," she ordered. "And shut your eyes."

He did it. Very slowly, but he did it. Terminal Sue moved around behind him, put the gun up against the back of his skull. "Put your hands on top of your head, Andrew Peak."

He did.

She pulled the cuffs out of her pocket, snapped them around his right wrist, keeping his hands up above his head, ran the chain over the pipe, above where it was riveted to the wall, and cuffed his left hand. Now he couldn't stand up without dislocating his shoulders.

"Keep your eyes shut," she ordered. She knew he wouldn't do it – they never did. "I'll be right back."

ANDREW PEAK KNELT in the corridor with his hands above his head. His shoulders had started hurting already, and he had only just been cuffed to the pipe.

He couldn't believe this was happening to him.

He'd actually been happy when the Indian had killed John, at the club. John, in the manner of bullies everywhere, had been tormenting Andrew his entire life, in ways petty and major. And Andrew had always liked the Renegade; he was sort of hoping to talk to the Indian about it.

And now she had him handcuffed to a pipe.

THERE WAS SERIOUS shit in the warehouse.

Shotguns and machine guns; mortars, bombs, plastic explosives; little rockets that looked like fourth of July specials, that Sue knew would take an airliner out of the sky.

Sue rifled the offices, tossing anything that looked interesting into a green trash bag. She'd look it over later, when she had more time. When she returned to the boy, he had his eyes open, of course. He shut them quickly at the sight of her.

"I saw that," Terminal Sue said. "You can open them now. You're a Nazi?"

"No," he lied. "I'm a secretary. I'm a secretary to the fellow who owns this place. I was here doing some late –"

Terminal Sue slapped him. Not hard, just hard enough to shut him up and get his attention, and she didn't feel the least bit guilty about it. She just pretended she was slapping Bogie. "Let's try again," she said gently. "I'm the Indian, and you know about a renegade, and you're a Nazi."

"I don't know anything," he repeated firmly.

Sue almost believed him. "Are you a Nazi?"

He stared at her. He opened his mouth once, closed it abruptly. "No. I'm –"

Terminal Sue didn't hit him this time. She pulled his head up by the hair and looked him in the eyes. "Look at me when you lie to me, Andrew."

Andrew's mouth tightened with sullen anger. This wasn't going the way he wanted it to. "Yes."

"Good boy. Are you a Nazi?"

"Yes, all right, yes. Are you happy? I'm a Nazi. I *was born* a Nazi, and I was raised a Nazi. Nobody asked me if I wanted to be a Nazi. It just happened. I'm a Capricorn, too. You got a problem with that?" Andrew had forgotten for an instant that he was chained to a pipe – and for a moment he had the oddest impression that the vicious Indian was about to laugh.

She *was* about to laugh. She knew it, man, she had just known it. If this nasty little Nazi bastard hadn't been spawned by the same Nazi clan that spawned Bogie, she would register Republican in the next election. "How many of you are there?"

"Ten of us." He sneered at her. "Seven, now. You've killed three. You killed Brian and John and Werner . . . not that any of them were losses," he muttered.

Terminal Sue crouched down so that she could look him in the eye, so that she was no longer looming over him. "Tell you what, Andrew. Maybe I'll let you live. You'd like that, wouldn't you?"

He grimaced. "I'd like anything that involves uncuffing me. My shoulders hurt."

"You're a whiner," Terminal Sue said. "And you're making this much too easy."

"I'm hungry," Andrew complained.

JUST AFTER FOUR A.M. Terminal Sue put Andrew, still handcuffed, into the passenger seat of her car. She drove to the end of the driveway that led away from the industrial park, and waited, watching her rear-view mirror.

At 4:11, as Sue was starting to wonder if she was going to have to go back inside and see what had gone wrong, the explosion came. From a hundred yards away the explosion rocked the car, and Terminal Sue felt the flash of heat against the back of her neck.

Terminal Sue, who was not impressed by very much, was impressed by the explosion. "Oh, my God," she said out loud. The fireball climbed upward, taking the warehouse's roof with it, throwing it up into the night sky, burning so fiercely that only seconds after the explosion it was uncomfortably warm –

"This warehouse park," said Terminal Sue out loud, "is going to burn down." She considered calling the fire department, but there was no point. Everyone within five miles of this was probably calling in alarms.

Andrew Peak leaned back in the passenger seat and shut his eyes. "I can't believe you did that."

Terminal Sue watched the flames. "Why not?"

"The security guard's office was behind our warehouse. He was an innocent man, and you killed him."

Terminal Sue turned her head and stared at him.

Kidnapped

THURSDAY MORNING, SHORTLY after dawn, well before Bogie's breakfast would have arrived and long before Bogie's doctor would have discharged him, Bogie slid out of his hospital bed, dressed himself awkwardly, one handed, in the clothes Dreadful Sam had left the night before, and escaped.

Bogie didn't know where Dreadful Sam had found the hat. It wasn't his; it was black, and it was a fedora, and it was the right size, but it wasn't Bogie's black fedora. It fit perfectly and it felt funny.

And the clothes. He didn't know where Dreadful Sam had gotten the clothes, either. They weren't his. They fit perfectly, the leather molded itself to him with none of the stiff new feel of clothing fresh off the rack, but the clothes weren't his either.

The nurse at the night desk tried to stop him. "Mister —" She glanced down at her bed chart, looked back up again. "Mr. Freedom? Where are you going?"

"Straight to Hell," Bogie said, because it amused him when Dreadful Sam said that. Bogie thought he was going to Heaven.

"You need to get back into bed, Mr. Freedom. The doctor will be here to see you about eleven, and you might even get out this afternoon. But you can't leave now. Someone shot you yesterday."

"Yes," Bogie agreed. "I was there." He wished Sue were here. He wouldn't let her actually shoot the nurse, but he'd let her threaten to shoot the nurse. "Oh, my God," said Bogie, pointing behind her. "Look at that!"

The nurse turned around to look.

Bogie turned and ran. He couldn't believe she'd fallen for that.

He heard noises behind him, and he assumed that the nurse was chasing him. Even shot in the shoulder, he thought, he could outrun a nurse.

"Mr. Freedom!" She was gaining on him. "Security!" she hollered.

Bogie glanced over his shoulder, yelled as loud as he could, "You're going to wake up your patients!" and darted into a stairwell. As the door closed, he heard buzzers.

He took the stairs two at a time, found himself slightly dizzy by the time he reached the ground floor. All this running and jumping had jarred his shoulder; he felt a dampness beneath the bandage covering his wound, and hoped that the blood wouldn't stain his new shirt.

He took a side corridor that led out into the parking lot, bypassing the admittance desk. In the lot, he wandered around looking for a car that he liked. He could hear shouts coming from the hospital, but ignored them. He was outside and they were inside.

And they couldn't keep him anyway, he hadn't done anything illegal. Or at any rate, nothing they knew about.

Well, nothing they could *prove*.

And besides, even if they could prove it, the hospital couldn't keep him. Hospitals couldn't keep you when you did illegal things. Only jails could.

He settled on a nice blue Ford. He liked Fords, and this one had a bumper sticker that said, *I'd rather be dead than drive a Chevy*. The Ford was a five-speed, which was rather awkward considering that he couldn't use his left arm, but he solved that problem quickly, steering with his left knee as he shifted, working the pedals with his right foot, and shifting with his right hand.

Once he got out onto the street, he was confronted with a dilemma. He couldn't go home; the Nazis knew where he lived, and Bogie expected they had the place wired to blow up the instant he opened the refrigerator door. He couldn't go to Terminal Sue's house; he didn't know where she lived. Dreadful Sam would lecture him about leaving the hospital too soon, Dave would complain about being woken up, Blue Hair would poke her finger in his wound –

He settled on Doctor Death and Kathy. Their front door was habitually unlocked; he could get in and be asleep on their couch, and they would probably never even notice.

He drove down the street, watching the eastern skyline grow pale.

Dawn looked different when you'd actually woken up for it.

KLAUS VODD, JEFF Stone and Claudia Hess halted in front of the old woman's house. Claudia, who was driving, hesitated before turning the engine off. Klaus and Jeff were out of the car and heading toward the house before she pulled the key from the ignition. This, she thought, was not such a great idea.

That old lady was a bitch.

"ANDREW PEAK," SAID Dreadful Sam. He looked at the young man, sitting on the sofa in Dreadful Sam's drawing room, hands cuffed behind his back. He had a fat lip. Dreadful Sam glanced at Terminal Sue in a disapproving fashion, and she looked, in response, more guilty than was normal for her. He hoped she hadn't done anything worse than what he saw before him – Dreadful Sam was hoping, once he got to Hell, to not know too many people there. "Susan says you're a Nazi."

The boy said in a surprisingly perky fashion, "Yes."

"Won't tell her where headquarters is, though."

Andrew Peak opened his mouth. Nothing came out.

Terminal Sue shrugged. "Somebody *did* something to him. I don't think he's messing with me; he *can't* tell me. I thought maybe he could tell you."

Dreadful Sam shook his head. "I'm not sure I care where their headquarters are."

Terminal Sue stared at him. "These people are bad news, Sam. They killed Carlo and they tried to kill Bogie. We –"

The blond boy on the couch said, "We didn't kill any damn security guards, though."

Dreadful Sam looked at the boy, looked at Terminal Sue's frozen features, and sighed. "I'll go make some tea," he said. Just at the moment he found it difficult to care that Terminal Sue preferred coffee.

THE OLD LADY lived in Brentwood, off of San Vicente avenue, in one of the old, cheaply built houses from the late '40s that had been intended for returning veterans of World War II. You'd been able to buy one for a thirty dollar down payment, Claudia had read, or a one dollar down payment if you were a veteran.

The woman's house was one of the nicer, better-cared for houses on the lot; it might not have been worth much when she and her husband purchased it fifty years ago, but it was worth an awful lot today. The car in the driveway was a silver Mercedes Benz; Claudia couldn't fault the woman's taste in cars.

Claudia and Jeff trailed around the house, to the back door, while Klaus rang the front door bell. Claudia thought the whole endeavor was pointless; the woman was a hundred years old. What was she going to do, run away?

They caught her slipping through her bedroom window, dressed in Nikes and black jogging sweats. Jeff pointed his gun at the woman and said, "Where do you think you're going?"

The woman smiled nastily, and said, "Jogging."

DOCTOR DEATH'S PHONE rang, and rang, and rang.

Eventually, Bogie opened his eyes, rolled off the couch, and picked it up. He had always suspected that Doctor Death and Kathy didn't answer their phone when they didn't feel like it.

It was Dreadful Sam. Again.

"I hate it when you do this," Bogie said.

"Do what?"

"Use the phone."

"We need to see you, Bogie. Come to my house."

"Why? You have more Nazis you want me to meet?"

"Just one," said Dreadful Sam. "He's in handcuffs on my front couch."

Bogie hung up the phone, slapped his hat back onto his head, and staggered out Doctor Death's front door.

A crow, a black crow, sat on her front step. Bogie hesitated, waiting to see what it would say.

It said nothing, of course.

"THANKS FOR THE fedora," said Bogie. "I like it," he lied.

Dreadful Sam nodded. "It belonged to Humphrey Bogart. He gave it to me so I could give it to you."

Bogie took the fedora off and looked at it. "Really? Me personally?"

Dreadful Sam said, "Well, I told him I had a friend who needed it."

Bogie spun the hat upside down, looking at it more closely. "My mother named me after Humphrey Bogart."

Dreadful Sam looked interested. "Really?"

Bogie, settling the hat back on his head, said, "I thought Bogart was a small man."

Dreadful Sam nodded. "He was. He just had a big head."

They were sitting at Dreadful Sam's kitchen table, drinking orange spice tea. Dreadful Sam had insisted that Terminal Sue stay in the living room with Andrew Peak. He was her Nazi, she could watch him.

"I really think we need to let him go," Bogie said.

"He's one of the bad guys," Dreadful Sam warned, "and they're after you."

"It's let him go," Bogie said, "or turn him over to the police, or kill him. If we turn him over to the police, we have to tell them Terminal Sue kidnapped him and blew up the warehouse. And I don't want to kill him. So I really think we should let him go."

Dreadful Sam bestowed one of his rare smiles on Bogie. "You're a good boy. I might see Terminal Sue on the other side, but I know I'm not going to see you again."

Bogie nodded. "I'm going to Heaven."

Terminal Sue and the Nazi were watching television when Bogie and Dreadful Sam entered the living room. Channel 2 Action News was showing footage of the burning warehouse. The reporter's voice ran over the video. "This is the site of last night's explosion at a warehouse rented by Fourth Kingdom Imports. So far there is only one known fatality, the park security guard. The guard's name is being withheld pending notification of his family."

For the first time since he had known her, Bogie Freedom felt sorry for Terminal Sue – she looked terrible. She turned off the television set. "They're not saying yet who the security guard was."

Neither Bogie nor Dreadful Sam said anything. Bogie couldn't think of anything to say, and all the things Dreadful Sam could think of, would have only made Terminal Sue feel worse.

"We're going to let him go," Bogie told Terminal Sue.

She looked at him for a moment, as though she wanted to protest, and then leaned down over Andrew Peak, ignoring his flinch, and unlocked the handcuffs. "Get the hell out."

CLAUDIA AND JEFF led Blue Hair back into her house. Claudia opened the front door for Klaus.

Klaus said, "How did you get in?"

"Through the bedroom window," said Claudia. "The old lady was slipping out the back. She must have seen us coming."

Blue Hair picked up her black stick, which was leaning in the corner of the living room, and smacked Jeff hard, on the button on the top of the Chicago Bulls baseball cap that he wore to hide his bald spot. He crumpled, 6'2" of blond muscle tumbling limply to the polished wooden floor.

Claudia and Klaus both leapt at the old woman. Klaus swung his fist at the old woman, and Claudia got a hold of the woman's shirt and yanked her back out of range. The woman was a hundred years old, for Christ's sake, Klaus would kill her. Klaus yanked the black stick, which Blue Hair still held, from her grip. He held it threateningly above her, and the old woman glared at him with an icy expression.

"You bitch," Klaus snarled.

"You," Blue Hair said, "will regret this."

Preparing To Rambo In Fontana

WALKIN' TALKIN' DAVE Bradden arrived at work seven hours early; he liked to be prompt.

He found, posted on the front door, a note:

> *Renegade – you have Andrew Peak. We have the old woman. Return Andrew to us personally, this evening at nine, at the Fontana office, and we will release the old woman. Don't show, and the old woman dies.*

There was a Fontana address, and below that it was signed, *Space Nazis from Hell*.

Walkin' Talkin' Dave thought that Claudia must have written the note. None of those other bastards had much of a sense of humor – fanaticism and humor didn't go together very well.

Dave let himself into *The Rock*, unlocking the many locks and turning off the alarm. He hesitated near the phone, and then called the hospital.

The line at the hospital rang three times before it was picked up. "ICU."

"I need to talk to Bogie Freedom," said Dave.

"Mr. Freedom released himself AMA."

AMA. Dave considered it; American Medical Association. Bogie released himself American Medical Association. It didn't make sense. "AMA?" he asked.

"Against medical advice," she said.

Dave nodded and hung up the phone. That sounded like Bogie. The only authority he could tolerate was Blue Hair's. He thought about who he should call next, but Bogie had ripped his phone out of the wall almost a month ago; he had no idea what Sue's telephone number was, and he was utterly unwilling to call the police. His immediate instinct was to call Blue Hair, but he assumed she must be the old woman in question.

On a sudden hunch he dialed Doctor Death's phone number. He knew it by heart.

A groggy voice answered. "Hello?"

"Doctor Death?" They sounded exactly alike on the phone.

"No, this is Kathy."

"Is Bogie there?"

"No –" There was a pause. "I think somebody took a nap on our couch. But it wasn't Bogie."

"How do you know?"

Kathy said with utter certainty, "Bogie wouldn't have come over here just to sleep by himself."

"He got shot," said Walkin' Talkin' Dave. "Maybe it slowed him down a little."

"Oh, wait . . . yep, it was Bogie," Kathy said. "There's blood on the couch."

"Is there a lot of blood?" Dave asked with concern.

"Not a whole lot. I've seen more."

The answer did not reassure Walkin' Talkin' Dave. "Okay. If you see him, let him know I'm looking for him, okay?"

"Sure." There was another pause, and then Kathy said, "You want to come over?"

Dave felt an excruciating pain. "I kind of gotta wait here for Bogie."

"Leave him a note," Kathy suggested.

"I can't," Walkin' Talkin' Dave protested. "Blue Hair's been kidnapped by Space Nazis from Hell, and I gotta take care of it first."

"Oh." Kathy hesitated and then said, "I thought you guys hated Blue Hair."

Dave, who didn't like to look like a liar, wanted to say that he did hate Blue Hair; but really, neither he nor Bogie hated Blue Hair. They just told people they did, because everything got back to Blue Hair eventually, and saying it behind her back was safer than saying it to her face. Besides, Dave and Bogie were convinced that Blue Hair said things about them behind *their* backs.

And she hit them with that stick, too.

Dave said, "Have Bogie call me if you see him," and hung up.

He wandered into the back room, to play *Space Nazis from Hell* and wait for someone to show up.

He fed a quarter into the machine, turned the brightness control down slightly, said, "Goddamn Nintendo," and started playing.

He hated those greedy corporate bastards. And he wasn't just saying that to get even because they were saying shit behind his back. As far as he knew, Nintendo had never said anything about him behind his back.

He hated them anyway.

BOGIE AND TERMINAL Sue arrived at two P.M. They were not speaking to one another. Bogie had insisted that they drive Andrew Peak back to Irvine, and drop him off exactly where Terminal Sue had taken him from. When she protested, he said piously, "You put things back where you got them."

Terminal Sue, who clearly recollected Bogie not putting any number of things back where he'd taken them from, wanted to shoot him – but she'd already killed too many people lately, and she refrained.

They both stopped at the front door and, in silence, together, read the note the Nazis had left.

Terminal Sue said out loud, "Space Nazis from Hell?"

Bogie Freedom said furiously, "They took Blue Hair." He hurried into the club, almost running back to Blue Hair's office. He snatched the handset to Blue Hair's old fashioned black phone up out of its cradle, quickly dialing a number. "Hi, Joanie. This is Bogie. Yeah, I need a chopper tonight. Urgent. Really important. I mean, a big chopper. Lots of space, it has to seat –" He looked around, at Terminal Sue, at Dave, who had just walked into Blue Hair's office, counting. "It has to handle five or six people at least. And some stuff. Lots of stuff. Okay, I'll wait." Bogie cradled the phone between his shoulder and his neck. "Dave, you know how to shoot a gun?"

Walkin' Talkin' Dave said, "Yeah, but I don't want to shoot a person. Not even a Space Nazi."

Bogie, who also refused to shoot Space Nazis, except on the video screen, said, "Don't worry about it. We can shoot over their heads, and if anybody needs to get really shot, Terminal Sue will do it."

Terminal Sue, who was tired of shooting people, wanted to protest. As she was opening her mouth, Walkin' Talkin' Dave said, "We could bring Doctor Death along. She would probably really shoot somebody."

Bogie nodded thoughtfully. A tinny voice said, "Bogie?"

Bogie slapped the handset up against his ear. "Yeah? What do you mean, I was supposed to fly on Tuesday? I never said I'd fly on Tuesday. I only fly on Mondays. Blue Hair only lets me off on Mondays. On Tuesdays I'm the Entertainment Director. Okay, yes, I do get mornings off. But I never made a commitment. Not a firm one . . . are you calling me a liar?"

The voice on the other end of the phone said something that Terminal Sue couldn't hear. It appeared to enrage Bogie. "I *paid* for that."

The voice on the other end went on for a while, and Bogie visibly calmed down. "Yeah, yeah, a Huey would be all right. But I want a big one. A scary one. With speakers. Big speakers mounted on it. Yeah, that's right. I want to play some Wagner as we come swooping in." Bogie paused. "No shit? You really met Marlon Brando once?" There was another long pause, and then Bogie said, "Yeah, and I'm wearing Humphrey Bogart's fedora. Big deal." Another pause, and Bogie said, "Six o'clock," and hung up.

He turned to Terminal Sue and Walkin' Talkin' Dave. "We pick the chopper up at six o'clock. They won't give us any speakers."

Walkin' Talkin' Dave nodded. "All right. I'm in." He turned to go. "Let me go call Doctor Death and Kathy."

Bogie said, "We're taking Kathy? Will she shoot somebody?"

Walkin' Talkin' Dave shrugged. "I don't know. But they do everything together. Doctor Death's going to refuse to fight Nazis if Kathy doesn't get to fight Nazis too." He left.

Terminal Sue said, "Who's going to fly the chopper?"

Bogie said, as though it were the most obvious thing in the world, "Me. It's what I do," he added, "when I'm not being the Entertainment Director."

Terminal Sue's eyes narrowed. "I thought you were a detective when you weren't the Entertainment Director."

"I am," Bogie said. "And I'm a damn fine one. Did you ever watch that show, *Magnum P.I.?* Remember how T.C. used to fly Magnum around, and then Rick used to run the restaurant? I do all that shit myself."

Terminal Sue said, "When do you find time to be a priest?"

Bogie shook his head. "Being a priest doesn't take a lot of time. Not like being a therapist. Man, psych patients can suck your blood."

Terminal Sue did not ask if he was a therapist, because of course he was, when he wasn't doing other things.

TERMINAL SUE TOOK down the note from the Nazis, turned it over, and wrote on the back, *The club will not be opening tonight. We regret the inconvenience.* She stuck it to the door.

When she went back inside, Bogie Freedom was standing in front of the video game, staring at it thoughtfully. Doctor Badoui's suggestion bounced around in the back of his head. He spun the brightness control – up, down. Up, down. He glanced around to see if anyone was watching; Terminal Sue turned her head the other direction as he glanced her way.

Almost furtively, Bogie slid his sunglasses down, and peered over them at the screen. He didn't take them all the way off . . . just lowered them a touch. "Damn," he murmured. He dug into his jeans, pulled out a quarter, and fed it into the machine.

He reached out one hand to punch the start button, glanced over at Terminal Sue, and said, "Blue Hair's been snatched. I need a moment alone."

Terminal Sue, who knew he was lying but couldn't figure out about what, glared at him. "We've got work to do," she said, stalling. "Have you ever assaulted a compound full of heavily armed fanatics? It's *hard* work. You can't just saunter in, rescue your hostages, and saunter back out again. You have to plan. Get weapons and ammunition. Do a tactical study of the site, make sure you're in good shape, do push-ups every morning..." She realized that she was babbling and shut up, but she refused to leave. Bogie was plotting something tricky, and she wanted to watch him do it. He wasn't a detective, or an Entertainment Director, or a pilot, or a priest or a therapist or any of those goddamn things, he was just a tricky Nazi bastard, and Terminal Sue didn't trust him at all.

"Uhm . . ." Bogie looked frantic. "Five minutes? Okay? I need five minutes by myself."

Terminal Sue said, "I'll turn my back."

"Okay," said Bogie. He watched her carefully, waiting for her to turn around.

She did so.

The *Space Nazis* game began beeping. "You're playing the fucking game," she said.

"I am not."

"I can hear it."

"It's a way to assuage my grief," said Bogie. "Keep your back turned."

Terminal Sue heard when his first man died. She heard the pause when his second man died. It seemed to take a very long time before the third man –

"Woohoo!"

Terminal Sue spun around.

Bogie Freedom, eyes firmly covered by his sunglasses, looked at her with a victorious expression. "You think you're so good," he sneered. He left the room without saying anything further.

The game's high score list no longer said TS ten times.

It said, BF, and then TS nine times.

The bastard had put the high score on the machine.

Terminal Sue dug into her jeans for some quarters.

BOGIE HURRIED INTO the bar. Dave was on the telephone. "Hey, Dave, guess what?"

Dave laid a hand over the mouthpiece, looking at Bogie inquiringly.

"Did you know you can see better without your sunglasses?"

Dave nodded. "Yeah. That's why I only wear mine when the sun's shining in my eyes." He returned to his conversation.

"You knew? You knew that?" Bogie stood motionless in front of the bar, staring at Dave. "Does *everybody* know that?"

"Yes," said Dave gently, covering the mouthpiece. "Everybody knows that, Bogie."

"Damn." Bogie never took his sunglasses off, because his mother had told him not to, and all her other advice had proven accurate, over the years. He wondered what else other people knew that he didn't know, but he couldn't imagine there was much. He peeped at Dave over the top of his sunglasses; the man was a lot lighter than Bogie had always thought. He thought about looking at other things without his sunglasses, and slid the sunglasses back up again. No point in overdoing it.

Bogie helped himself to a Budweiser, and settled down at the bar.

From the back room came the sound of the video game.

Dave said into the phone, "Yeah, Fontana. Do you have a gun . . . yeah, I kind of thought you did." He told Bogie, "Doctor Death and Kathy are in. They want to know if they should wear ninja outfits."

Bogie shrugged. "Tell them to wear whatever they want, as long as it's black."

Dave said, "Bogie says wear whatever you want, as long as it's black. Okay, sure, hang on a second." He said to Bogie, "Kathy wants to know if you think they have no fashion sense at all? They know what to wear to go Rambo in Fontana."

Bogie nodded. He had never doubted it.

Dave hung up the phone, and made a series of calls, telling the other bartenders, bouncers, cocktail servers, and doormen not to show up for work. He tried to call the band, but couldn't get a hold of them at the only number he had; he called their agent, and left a message for them there. Finally, he hung up the phone and got his own beer.

"Blue Hair's not going to like this when she finds out," he said.

"It's either this or let her die," said Bogie.

Blue Hair *wasn't* going to like it, though.

He imagined she was in a foul mood, right about now.

Ramboing In Fontana

BLUE HAIR, STILL in her black sweat suit, was tied to a chair. She sat with perfect posture, her gimlet eyes watching Jessica, the young woman they'd left to guard her. Jessica had begun avoiding her eyes.

"The problem with you people," said Blue Hair severely, "is that you have no sense of history."

Jessica had been told by Claudia, who had had the misfortune to actually speak to Blue Hair, not to respond to any conversational gambits.

"You *lost*," Blue Hair continued. Blue Hair smiled her cold, hateful smile. "My son and millions of others like him went to war and *beat* your Kaiser, that pathetic Adolph Shicklegruber. The man was illegitimate, you do realize, not at all entitled to the name he chose to call himself by. But really, Heil Shicklegruber simply doesn't have that ring to it, does it?"

Jessica said stiffly, "Hitler failed because he was betrayed by the inferior races, the mud people."

Blue Hair's hateful smile grew wider. "He was *beaten* by the 'mud people.'"

Jessica leaned forward, meeting the old woman's eyes. *"We're not going to fail. We've learned from the lessons of history. We won't strike before we're ready, and when we do strike, it will be from a direction none of you expect."

"Lessons of history," Blue Hair mused. "I take it, my dear, that's a euphemism for mistakes of the past." The girl didn't respond, and Blue Hair continued. "You're going to try to take over what? Los Angeles? The United States? The world? You've saddled yourself with a heritage that's hated by people around the globe, in every country including your own. If –"

Jessica laughed at her. "Nobody in *my* country hates our heritage, old woman."

Blue Hair gazed at her thoughtfully. There were two groups involved here, Blue Hair had come to realize. The skinheads, the locals, were the first and much larger group. Blue Hair had seen several of them on the way into the compound, had seen them get chased out of the quarters they were currently holding her in. The second group was much smaller; she had only seen four of them so far. The three who had taken her; Klaus, Claudia, and the one she'd hit on his Chicago Bulls cap, Jeff. Klaus spoke English with a faint German accent, and German with a faint American accent. Claudia spoke perfect American English and perfect German German; this Jessica spoke only English, as far as Blue Hair could tell. By the accent, Blue Hair would have guessed she came from some Southwestern state. She had a hint of that cowboy twang associated with the Southwest.

And nobody in *their* country hated Nazis.

Blue Hair wished she were free. She wished she had her stick.

She wished Dave and Bogie and that nice young Indian girl would get here soon. Blue Hair wondered if the Indian girl would like a job; perhaps Head Bouncer. Not that Bogie was bad at it; he was the best bouncer Blue Hair had ever had. But Blue Hair suspected that with the Indian girl as Head Bouncer, nobody would ever need to get bounced. The Indian girl would simply intimidate them into line.

Blue Hair admired that in a person.

WALKIN' TALKIN' DAVE Bradden, Doctor Death and Kathy assembled themselves in the passenger compartment of the Huey just after seven-thirty P.M. Bogie seated himself in the pilot's seat. He liked being a helicopter pilot. Pretending to be a small plane pilot was all right, but pretending to be a helicopter pilot was a lot better. Helicopters could land anywhere. Bogie winced, remembering. Well, almost anywhere.

Being a jet pilot, now – that sucked. You were trapped in a little compartment with a bunch of dials, and you never got to dip or dive or spin or turn. And there were always other people trying to tell you what to do. For commercial airlines, anyway. Bogie suspected that being a jet pilot in one of those little tiny fast fighter planes that the United States government owned would be much better. But you had to join the Armed Forces to fly one of those, and that was where Bogie drew the line. Bogie had never joined anything in his life, and he didn't intend to start just so that he could fly a fighter jet. Still, maybe if he could … liberate one of those jets.

Terminal Sue climbed up into the front compartment and strapped herself into the seat next to Bogie. She looked at him with black Indian eyes – she'd taken her sunglasses off.

Bogie kept his on. It was still daylight, after all. He looked at Terminal Sue. "How hard do you think it would be to get onto an Air Force base?"

Terminal Sue said shortly, "Military jets are really well guarded, Bogie."

Bogie stared at her.

Terminal Sue said, "I can read you like a book," which was true and was starting to scare her. "Are we going to take off?"

"Yeah." Bogie started the engine. He didn't care how well guarded those jets were. He had Terminal Sue, and she had guns. Bogie thought that with Terminal Sue's help, he could get in anywhere.

They lifted up out of Van Nuys airport, and headed east, fleeing the setting sun.

FONTANA IS A small town in Southern California, known principally for the Kaiser Fontana hospital located there. Once there had been a Kaiser Steelworks, but it had been shut down long ago, and all the laborers thrown out of work. Today there were almost as many skinheads as there were unemployed.

The 10 Freeway bisected the city; Terminal Sue manned the Thomas Guide, and Bogie flew down the length of the freeway, periodically dipped down low enough to take a look at the freeway signs. He took the exit Terminal Sue told him to take, flying south out over a desolate, industrial area filled with junk yards and the rusting hulks of ancient trains.

"We're coming up on the address," Terminal Sue called back to the three in the passenger compartment. "Is everyone armed?"

Dave said, "I'm not. I refuse to shoot anyone."

Terminal Sue looked at him sourly. "Carry one for appearance's sakes, okay?" She turned to Bogie. "Is your gun loaded?"

Bogie said, "Nope."

Kathy held her AK-47 up. "Totally empty."

Terminal Sue unslung her backpack. "Fortunately," she said, "I brought ammunition for everyone." She spilled out an amazing collection of ammo onto the deck of the Huey. "You don't have to shoot anyone, just point the guns in the air and use them to make noise, okay?" She started sorting the ammo out into groups. "These are .38 specials. These go to the two AK-47s. These go into my .44 magnum, and these boxes are for the nine millimeter autos."

"It's against the law to shoot into the air," Kathy observed. "The bullets come back down and hit children. Sometimes they die, and sometimes they're only blinded. Besides, what if there's a ricochet problem?"

"You just fire that rifle," said Terminal Sue. "I know everyone expects me to do all the hard work, but at least *try* and look intimidating."

Doctor Death said, offended, "Hey! I'll kill people. I'll kill as many people as *you* do."

"I thought you only killed people who deserved it," said Terminal Sue. She was in a foul mood on the whole subject of killing people, lately.

Doctor Death looked surprised. "They're Nazis, and they snatched Blue Hair. Of course they deserve it."

Terminal Sue nodded. She had a point. The Nazis did deserve it. It wasn't like they were talking about a bunch of innocent security guards. "Okay. But don't shoot anyone who doesn't shoot at us, first."

"Naturally."

Bogie turned to look at Terminal Sue in surprise. "I thought you'd shoot anyone."

Terminal Sue turned back to him while the others loaded up. "I shot two people," she said in a rage that had been building all day. "Two people, in my whole stinking life, before I met you. And I've killed four people in the last four days, even if one of them was an accident, and if I get any more shit from you about it, I might kill *you*." She settled back in her seat, staring at the well lit tangle of buildings looming up ahead of them.

Bogie glared at her, not looking where he was flying. He wanted to continue the argument; he wasn't really afraid she would kill him, not any more. But he was afraid he would never get onto an Air Force base if he alienated Terminal Sue. "Okay," he said finally, in his best therapist's voice. "You're entitled to your feelings."

"You try and play therapist with me," snapped Terminal Sue, "and I'll smack you so hard your head turns around."

Bogie shut up and concentrated on flying the helicopter. He had conciliatory and forgiving things he wanted to say in his priest voice, but he was afraid to. He thought she might recognize the voice, and it would just piss her off worse.

Terminal Sue pointed. "That's it. That's the compound."

"Compound" was the correct word. Eight or nine buildings, built like bunkers, with tall fences surmounted by razor wire. It looked like a military position that its holders expected to have to defend from a heavy infantry attack. Small towers rose up at each of the four corners of the enclosed area. Nobody stood atop them, but they looked suspiciously like guard towers to Terminal Sue, early warning stations to alert the Nazis in the event somebody tried to do what they were doing right now. She wondered why there was nobody atop them, and then had to stop wondering: the helicopter lurched sickeningly, dropped down out of the sky like a stone –

Shrieks came from the back of the Huey. Terminal Sue heard herself scream.

The helicopter came to a solid, thudding landing.

Bogie smiled at her. "When you land it like that, they can't shoot at you."

"I want to kill you," said Terminal Sue, and she wasn't joking.

"And if there's anyone on the ground where you want to land," said Bogie, still smiling, still pleased with himself, "they run away, really fast. Because they're afraid you'll crush them. Like in the Wizard of Oz, when the witch –"

Terminal Sue hissed, "I swear to *God*, some day I really am going to kill you. You're asking for it if anyone is."

"I'll deal with you later," said Bogie Freedom. "Let's go rescue Blue Hair."

As they all piled out of the helicopter, Terminal Sue said, "We need to leave somebody here to guard the helicopter."

Bogie leaned back into the helicopter and yanked the keys out of the ignition. "Come on," Bogie said. "We're looking for someplace nice."

Terminal Sue glanced at him. "Nice?"

"Sure," said Bogie. "Blue Hair likes nice environments."

"I don't think," said Terminal Sue, and then hit the ground as a bullet whined by her ear. *"Show time!"*

Only she and Doctor Death fired their weapons. Bogie lowered himself to the ground next to Terminal Sue, rather slowly Sue thought; Sue heard Kathy and Dave going down. "You know how to shoot that gun?" Terminal Sue asked. She squeezed off a round in the direction of the shapes, scrambling among the buildings, that were shooting at them. Somebody screamed.

Bogie looked at the automatic doubtfully. "I could figure it out."

"Shoot the lights," said Terminal Sue. "Point it at the lights and pull the trigger." She squeezed off another round with the magnum, aiming high to compensate for windage. Another shape staggered and went down.

Bogie aimed carefully and squeezed the trigger. Nothing happened.

"Take the safety off," Terminal Sue snapped.

Bogie began examining his automatic carefully. Terminal Sue reached over and slapped the safety off, and then, because she could, slapped the back of Bogie's head too. "Start shooting lights if you don't want to die."

Bogie fired, and shot out a light. *"Woohoo!"* It was exactly the same noise he'd made when he got the high score on *Space Nazis*.

A bullet hit the ground a foot in front of Bogie's face. Dirt exploded into his eyes.

Terminal Sue said, "Don't make noises. It tells them where you are."

Bogie wiped dirt out of his face. This sucked. This sucked worse than being a chauffeur. He aimed carefully, shot out three more floodlights, and plunged the compound into darkness. He leapt to his feet, shouted, "Come on," to his many followers, and charged toward the buildings.

Terminal Sue *did* follow, running at top speed. Bogie was pulling away from her, the bastard could run faster than she could; she wondered what he thought he was going to do when he reached the people who were shooting at him, the people he didn't intend to shoot back at. Bogie rounded a corner, ahead of Terminal Sue, and vanished from her sight –

Terminal Sue skidded around the corner. Bogie was smacking some blond dude in the side of the head with his gun. He was holding another blond skinhead down on the ground with one foot, while a third blond dude rolled around clutching his genitals.

The blond dude Bogie had smacked collapsed into the dirt. The third guy squirmed free from beneath Bogie's foot; Terminal Sue kicked him sharply behind the ear. He collapsed limply to the ground.

Bogie said in a breathless voice, *"This* is what being a bouncer is all about. How many more do you think there are?"

"How should I know?" They were joined by the other three.

Dave said, "If we had a guy at the gate, counting them as they came in, we would know."

"You guys have worked in a club too long," said Terminal Sue.

Doctor Death said, "We only let 270 people into our restaurant."

Kathy frowned. "You don't actually think there's 270 Nazis here?"

"No," said Doctor Death. "There –"

Terminal Sue snapped, "You three take the buildings on the left. Bogie and I will take the buildings on the right. Doctor Death, make sure you kill anyone who tries to kill the three of you, okay?"

Walkin' Talkin' Dave looked at the three blond dudes with buzz cuts Bogie had laid out. "I could do this kind of thing," he offered.

Terminal Sue said, *"Go."*

MOMENTS AFTER THE gunfire erupted, in the nicest room in the compound, the room with curtains, Blue Hair said to Jessica, *"That is my Entertainment Director, my Bar Manager, and my potential Head Bouncer."*

Jessica shrugged. "We have a dozen men here, and they're all armed. Your people aren't going to get very far."

"My potential Head Bouncer," Blue Hair said gleefully, "is going to come in here and shoot you."

The first volley of shots ceased. Jessica waited. There were no further shots, not immediately, and Jessica nodded. "I expect that was them, getting shot," she told the old woman. "I hope you won't mind being buried in a mass grave. If the Renegade went down, we have no reason to keep you alive."

Blue Hair felt a flicker of fear. She refused to spend eternity in a grave with Walkin' Talkin' Dave Bradden and Bogie Freedom. She expected their graves to be near hers, of course, but not the *same* grave. "I expect to outlive you by a good bit," she said with as much fierceness as she could muster.

"I doubt it," said Jessica. She produced a small handgun, a .38 revolver, and pointed it at Blue Hair. "I hear anyone getting close to us, and I'm going to shoot you."

Two gunshots, one after another, exploded somewhere nearby.

A body crashed into the door behind Jessica.

Jessica looked startled, turned to look at the door, turned back to point the gun at Blue Hair as the door slammed open, a tall blond man fell backward through it, and the Indian woman who had just shoved him shot Jessica in the back of the skull.

Blue Hair watched Jessica fall and then looked up at the Indian girl. "Would you like a job, dear?"

Bogie Freedom, lying on the floor just inside the door, rolled over onto his back. "Don't fall for it," he warned Terminal Sue. "The only time she'll ever be nice to you is when she offers you the job."

"Mr. Freedom," said Blue Hair, "that is *not* your hat."

A Real American Hero

"It belongs to Humphrey Bogart," said Bogie. "I'm borrowing it."

"I thought I recognized it," said Blue Hair as Terminal Sue used a big Rambo knife to cut through the bonds holding Blue Hair to the chair. Blue Hair gave Bogie the evil eye as Terminal Sue released her, and Bogie, staggering to his feet, trying not to use his left arm too much, cursed the treacherous Indian; he knew he would never hear the end of this from Blue Hair. He'd be hearing for years about how she'd had to wait for the Indian girl to release her, while Bogie lounged there on the floor.

Terminal Sue took a moment to examine their surroundings. Office space; desks, a safe against one wall –

She pointed the Rambo knife at the safe and said to Bogie, "Open that."

Bogie glanced at Blue Hair. "I . . . I . . . I don't have the combination."

Terminal Sue said, "She doesn't know you open things?"

"I'm the Entertainment Director. I don't need to open things."

Blue Hair said, "Open the safe, Mr. Freedom."

Bogie opened the safe.

Terminal Sue said to Blue Hair, "Did you know he's a car thief?"

WHEN THE ACTION started, Alec Armstrong came through the main gate at eighty miles an hour. The car punched the gate off its hinges, with the car itself suffering only cosmetic damage; Armstrong whipped the wheel to the left, to run down one of the fleeing gate guards. He immediately whipped it back to the right, to avoid ramming the helicopter. The car slewed around to a stop, and Armstrong leaped out.

He held an Army issue .45 revolver in each hand, and unlike Bogie, Dave, and Kathy, was perfectly prepared to shoot Nazis. He was perfectly prepared to shoot practically anyone, and unlike Terminal

Sue, he wouldn't suffer a lot of guilt over it. Armstrong had killed a *lot* of Nazis, in his time.

The main fighting seemed to be going on over at the west wing; Alec ran in that direction. He barreled around the corner Bogie Freedom had taken only minutes before, stopping long enough to shoot the three wounded skinheads, and put them down for good. He moved slowly, cautiously, toward the largest building in the complex, some sort of warehouse, the only building that had noise coming from it: a fusillade of gunshots followed by a "Fuck! Those Nazi bastards shot me!"

Armstrong slid along the side of the building, slowly edging closer until he could risk a quick glance through the window. He had a perfect view of three . . . non-Nazis, he presumed. They were crouched behind a stack of crates. Two of them were shooting into the air; the third was carefully examining the hole someone had put into a nice black leather jacket. "Fucking Nazis," the girl said again. "Goddamn seven hundred dollar leather coat." The girl carefully shot a baseball cap off one of the Nazi heads.

Armstrong took another quick glance around the compound; nobody moving outside. He looked back inside, a long enough look to get the positions of everyone inside, both the Nazis and the . . . whatever they were.

The girl shot somebody in the boot, wounding the finely tooled leather. "Take that," she screamed. "If you bastards dressed better I'd show you some *real* shooting!"

The door, slightly ajar, was positioned between the Nazis and the non-Nazis. Entering the warehouse would put Armstrong into the line of fire of both parties – but the girl in the leather jacket seemed to have good aim, and was only shooting clothing, and the other two were only shooting the roof.

Alec Armstrong dived through the door, landing on his right shoulder, on the cement floor, rolling through it and rising to his feet in one smooth, quick motion. A bullet caught him in the center of his chest, in the center of his bullet-proof vest; Alec tried to ignore the sledgehammer impact and started shooting. It took him five shots. Four Nazis, five shots; his first shot, fired as he took a step backward under the impact of the bullet, missed. Armstrong did not aim at their chests and the next four shots did *not* miss.

Armstrong spun around, pointing his guns at the three left alive.

"Alec Armstrong," he said. "CIA."

The girl who'd been shooting people in the clothes said admiringly, "A real American hero."

The young man said to her, "Shoot *his* clothes."

"They're old," she said. "Off the rack. It won't hurt him."

BOGIE HELD THE door for Blue Hair, as they left the building. Blue Hair refused to run; she walked to the helicopter, with Bogie a step behind, and Terminal Sue behind them both, facing backward, ready to shoot anyone with bad enough judgment to come after them.

Bogie glared at the back of Blue Hair's blue hair. She had a jogging suit on, why weren't they running? Bogie handed her up into the helicopter, ignoring the ugly old blue Buick that had suddenly parked itself next to the chopper. "You keep her safe," said Terminal Sue. "Shoot people if you have to. I'm going to go get Dave and the girls."

Bogie climbed into the pilot's seat; Blue Hair took the seat next to it, the one Terminal Sue had used on the way out. Bogie started the engine. Shoot people, he thought. It wasn't something he did.

Someone began shooting at *them*. A bullet starred the Huey's windshield. Terminal Sue, standing outside, started shooting back. Bogie thought it was taking her an awful long time to make whoever it was who was shooting at them *stop* shooting at them; *another* bullet struck the windshield, shattering it completely. Then the shooting ceased, and Terminal Sue waved at him, and took off at a run toward the west side of the compound.

At the far side of the compound, standing next to the gate, a man raised a rocket launcher to his shoulder. Bogie saw the man lifting it, raising it toward the chopper; a rocket streaked away from the far side of the compound. The blades were up to speed; Bogie lifted the helicopter a dozen feet off the ground.

The rocket hit the Buick. It exploded violently, the fireball rocking the Huey. The Huey slipped in the air, dropped several feet as Bogie fed gas to the engine . . . and the Huey bounced back up into the air again.

"I understood you could control this conveyance, Mr. Freedom," Blue Hair said severely.

TERMINAL SUE BURST into the warehouse, hit the ground rolling, and came up with her gun pointed at the back of Alec Armstrong's skull.

"Don't shoot!" Dave yelled. "He's a . . . he's not an enemy."

Alec Armstrong turned to face Terminal Sue's gun. "You're Susan Walks-Far," he said. "I'm Alec Armstrong. I've been wanting to talk to you."

Terminal Sue lowered her gun; this was the man Dreadful Sam had warned her about. "Come on," she told the others. "We've got Blue Hair. Let's get out of here."

The chopper landed on the pavement outside the warehouse, the cargo door sliding open. Bogie yelled, "Come on!"

With the exception of Alec Armstrong, they all ran toward the helicopter, scrambling up into the cargo compartment. Bogie leaned out, and hollered to Alec Armstrong, "Do you own a blue Buick?"

Armstrong stood in the doorway, watching his Buick burn. "Not any more." He followed the non-Nazis into the helicopter, not scrambling, not running. He wouldn't have minded if someone had showed up to continue the fire fight; that Buick had been a good car.

Terminal Sue leaned out of the chopper when Armstrong was close enough, grabbed him by his bullet proof vest, and hauled the old man into the chopper as Bogie lifted into the sky. "You fucking idiot!" she screamed at him. "There's a man with a goddamn rocket launcher at the gate, and you're keeping us sitting on the ground!"

Armstrong shook her hands off, settled back on the long bench. Amateurs always got excited. "What are you people doing here, anyway?" He glanced up front, at the old woman with the blue hair, then back to Susan Walks-Far. "This is no place for amateurs."

Walkin' Talkin' Dave said, "They snatched Blue Hair. She's our leader. We had to get her back."

Bogie yelled back, "The checks are no good if she doesn't sign them."

Armstrong nodded. "You can be pleased with the way this has turned out," he said. "You had no business flying into a compound where you were outnumbered thirteen to five, and successfully rescuing this woman without professional help." He paused. "Well, you had professional help, at the end."

"Thirteen?" said Dave.

Alec Armstrong said, "I was parked down the street, watching the gate with binoculars. I counted them as they went in."

Walkin' Talkin' Dave said to Terminal Sue, "You see? A professional killer, and *he* counted them on the way in. And you sneered when I suggested it." He looked at Doctor Death. "I knew we should have brought one of the doormen, and posted him at the gate."

"Next time," said Doctor Death.

Terminal Sue ignored them all. She had her backpack open and was counting the stacks. Hundred dollar bills, bundled in collections of fifty each.

"How much?" asked Alec Armstrong.

"I don't know," said Terminal Sue. "It's all in hundreds. It's a lot. I picked it up for the family of this security guard I know."

"We could use it," said Armstrong, "in the Cause." You could hear the capital letter on the word. "It would pay for –"

"What cause?" Kathy asked. She liked causes; save the whales, save the seals, save the environment.

Terminal Sue closed the backpack and set it on the deck behind her. "You touch it," she said grimly, "and I'll shoot you."

Nobody, least of all Alec Armstrong, doubted her for an instant.

The helicopter droned on into the night.

BOGIE PUT THE chopper down in the rear parking lot at *The Rock*. He sighed with relief when the chopper finally settled; he hadn't been able to see clearly for the last twenty minutes. Red spots kept dancing in front of his eyes. He hadn't told anybody; there was no point in worrying them. His shoulder was bleeding again; the blood had soaked through his shirt, staining the leather of his vest. It was the left shoulder, out of the line of everyone's sight. No one had noticed. He sat in the pilot's seat while everybody else got out of the chopper, then unbuckled himself and tried to stand up, and almost made it.

He sank back into the seat to rest for a minute.

Terminal Sue, Blue Hair, and Alec Armstrong disappeared into the restaurant. Dave leaned his head back into the chopper, and said, "If you need me, I'll be at Doctor Death's and Kathy's."

"They say," Bogie could hear Kathy saying, "that almost getting killed makes you, you know, well, *extremely* –"

Her voice trailed off into the distance.

Bogie sat bleeding in the pilot's seat and felt betrayed. He hated them, he thought. He hated them all. He sat in the quiet, listening to the traffic out on Sunset Boulevard, hating the world.

Terminal Sue appeared in the cargo entry. "Are you coming?"

Bogie looked at her. "Traitor."

Terminal Sue climbed into the cargo space, so she could get her face up close to Bogie's. "Listen, you dumb –" She stopped. "Is that your blood? Christ, it smells like a butcher shop in here. Did you get shot?"

"Yes!" Bogie yelled.

Terminal Sue looked at him with great concern. She said gently, "Where?"

"In the shoulder."

"Again?"

"No, you traitor, it's the same old shot. Yesterday's shot. Maybe when you get shot it heals up in one day. Me, it takes at least two."

"Christ," swore Terminal Sue. "Let's get you inside." She helped him to his feet, and half-carried him out of the Huey. "You better not bleed on me, either."

Her shirt was already splotched with Bogie's blood.

BLUE HAIR HANDED Bogie a tall glass filled with something unidentifiable. Bogie eyed it suspiciously. "What's this?"

"It will help you replace the fluids you lost, Mr. Freedom. I suggest you drink it."

"What's *in* it?"

"Pedialyte, grapefruit juice, and Malibu rum."

Bogie took a sip. "Tastes good."

Blue Hair nodded. "And good for you."

Terminal Sue said, "What's Pedialyte?"

"One uses it on infants," said Blue Hair. "When they have diarrhea, the Pedialyte replenishes the body fluids they've lost. It works well on gunshot victims, too."

"You keep this drug for infants behind the bar, at a club that caters to metalheads?" asked Terminal Sue politely.

Blue Hair shrugged. "One learns to be prepared." She turned to Alec Armstrong. "Now. If you wouldn't mind telling me, young man" – Armstrong was seventy if he was a day; Blue Hair was still old enough to be his mother – "what exactly were you doing at the Nazi compound?"

"I'll tell you," said Armstrong, "but first, I have to briefly explain the complete history of the world up to this point."

The Complete History Of
The World Up To This Point

"IMAGINE 1955," ALEC Armstrong said softly.

Terminal Sue didn't even give it a chance. "Can't."

Bogie said, "Beaver."

Terminal Sue, who had never been much of a television watcher, thought he was saying something derogatory about women. She turned on him and said furiously, "You watch your filthy mouth."

Blue Hair said, "I always hated that little boy."

Bogie said, *"My* filthy mouth? What the hell did I say?"

Blue Hair said, almost apologetically, "A television show, dear. 'Leave It To Beaver.' It was on the air in the 1950s. Mr. Freedom is knowledgeable on such subjects. I, unfortunately, lived through that era."

Bogie didn't like the way she kept calling Terminal Sue 'dear.' They seemed to be bonding. Blue Hair was *his* employer, and even if he hadn't known her as long as Terminal Sue had known Dreadful Sam, he had certainly known her far longer than Terminal Sue had.

"1955," said Alec Armstrong, apparently determined to keep the conversation on course. "In New Mexico. I was thirty years old, and I was working for the CIA...."

ALEC ARMSTRONG SHIVERED in the cold night air.

He lay on the hill in the darkness, overlooking the construction site. His superiors had been very clear: he was not to attempt to penetrate the site. He was merely to observe, and to report back in the morning.

There were Nazis down there.

Not many real Nazis, to be sure. Most of them were Americans. But enough of them were Germans, legally let into the country by the American government, to enrage Armstrong. It wasn't even out of the ordinary; ever since the end of the War the government had been granting citizenship, and new papers, to Nazis, mostly scientists and ex-intelligence agents, whom the government thought might be useful. His own superiors had set up any number of Nazis in comfortable new positions in the United States. The government had supplied them with jobs, homes, cars and money.

It had enraged Armstrong the first time he'd heard of such a case. It had never ceased to enrage him. Armstrong had fought in the war. Just barely; he'd turned 18 at the tail end of 1944 and had enlisted. He had seen only two months of combat before VE-Day, and had spent the rest of his tour in Germany, cleaning up after the Nazis. What they'd done to their own people was dreadful, but what they'd done to the Jews and Gypsies, homosexuals and cripples, the politically unreliable, and anyone else they didn't like, had surpassed belief. Armstrong had been among the first American soldiers at not one, but two concentration camps.

In Germany, he had learned compassion. He had had to come home, and find the Nazis on his own land, before he learned hate.

He raised the binoculars to his eyes and peered down into the construction site. The bustle of activity visible earlier in the day had slowed as night approached. He didn't know for sure what the Nazis were building down there, but he had his suspicions, and they were dire. Two of the scientists down there had been involved in Germany's atomic energy program; a third had been instrumental in designing the V-2 rockets that had hammered London.

Trucks had been delivering supplies to the site for weeks; enough supplies to keep the four hundred people working at the site alive for years. Food, and water. *Incredible* amounts of water.

Alec Armstrong's superiors thought the Germans were working under their supervision. They thought they knew what was going on down there.

Alec Armstrong thought they were wrong. He lay on the frozen ground, peering down into the camp. The problem was not that something was wrong. The problem lay in convincing the people who could *do* something about it. If they would –

The lights came on over the rows of worker housing, at the edge of the construction site. This was something new; the exterior lights generally went off at ten P.M. and didn't come back on again until sundown the next day.

For the next half hour, Armstrong watched what looked like an evacuation. For the most part it seemed orderly enough . . . but where the hell were they going? He watched them abandoning the houses, heading for the main building, and vanishing inside. He glanced at his watch – 12:12 A.M. – and, using his penlight to see the paper, wrote in his notebook, *Massive personnel movement. Congregating in main building. ?? Makes no sense. 400+ workers at site; can't fit them all in building.*

By 12:30, the site appeared deserted. Four hundred men, women, and children, had gone into a building that would not hold them. Alec climbed to his feet. His superiors had forbidden him, in writing, to go down there.

Armstrong started down the hill. He stopped, midway down, to take another pair of photographs of the deserted site.

The main building disintegrated.

It fell apart in stages; first the very top peeled off, followed by the walls, falling outward in a graceful, apparently planned collapse.

Armstrong began taking pictures as rapidly as his camera would allow. There was a pause once the building had collapsed, and Armstrong, who still had two pictures left on the roll, was wise enough to pop it out and replace it with a fresh roll.

Where the building had been, a gaping black hole lay exposed. The hole widened as Armstrong watched . . . the edges caving in, dropping down into the darkness. Armstrong took pictures. He'd never seen anything like it before, not during the War, not ever.

He heard the roar before he saw anything. He wished he had a tape recorder so that he could document the sound; it was a rumble so deep it shook the ground Armstrong stood on.

Light flooded the desert. It struck out from the huge hole in the ground, like a searchlight pointed upward. Armstrong shielded his eyes, still snapping photographs, holding the camera to one side and shooting into the glare until the glare had grown so bright there was no point to it any longer.

The rockets came up out of the glare.

The afterimage was imprinted on Armstrong's retinae for hours afterward. It was the brightest thing he'd ever seen, as bright as the noon-day sun. They came up together, five of them, lifting into the night sky, changing it to day. A dry heat radiated out across the desert, washed over Armstrong –

The Geiger detector he'd brought with him started chattering. Armstrong couldn't hear it, couldn't hear anything over the sound of the rockets.

The five ships disappeared into the night, the light slowly fading behind them.

It was dark again when Armstrong turned and ran. He ran the four miles back to his car, scrambling into the back seat. Out of breath, still half-blind from the rocket glare, he fumbled at the portable radio that was there, finally connecting with the operator back at base. "This is Armstrong, out at the site," he gasped. "We just had rockets take off from the site. No, damn it, I'm not crazy, I'm not drunk, I have photos, I saw it happen, get the Air Force and have them track it, *I want to know where these people are going!*"

ARMSTRONG SAID, "THEY went to Venus."

Blue Hair's eyes narrowed. "Venus," she said, "is uninhabitable. The air is not breathable; the atmospheric pressure is immense. It's lethally hot."

"Do you recall Biosphere II?" Armstrong asked. "It was an attempt, a while back, to create a totally artificial and self-sustaining environment. Eight people lived there for a year. Decades before, the United States government funded a similar attempt. You've never heard about it. Nazi scientists were experimenting with artificial environments. Back in the early 1950s they proposed to build a totally artificial underground environment in which to live – as a way to protect the President in the event of nuclear war. That's what was supposed to be happening, out there in the desert." Armstrong shook his head. "Obviously, that's not what really happened. Four hundred American and German Nazis built five spaceships, and went to Venus. They didn't know what Venus was like, back then; they didn't know what they were getting into. We thought they'd died. Obviously, at least some of them survived. Five years ago, we tracked a rocket ship returning from Venus." Armstrong smiled mirthlessly. "That was the first indication we had that they'd survived, despite the passage of close to thirty-five years. The agent on that rocket – the Nazi that the others have been calling the Renegade – must have thought he'd landed in paradise. I suspect that Venus must seem a close approximation of Hell."

There was a silence that lasted only a moment, and then Bogie and Terminal Sue said simultaneously, "Space Nazis from Hell."

Space Nazis From Hell

THE CAR PHONE rang twice before Claudia got it off the hook. Klaus, in the passenger's seat, didn't move. He stared straight ahead as the phone rang, in a withdrawn, uncommunicative rage.

She took the phone off the hook with her right hand, steering with the tips of her left fingers. It sent a wave of shock up through the left arm. Her left arm was virtually worthless; the bullet had passed completely through it, luckily missing the bone. It was bandaged and immobile. She quickly tucked the phone in between her neck and shoulder. "Hello?"

"Claudia?" It was Andrew.

"Andrew," she said quickly, "where are you?" She had a fondness for the boy that she wouldn't usually admit to; even in the midst of what appeared to be complete catastrophe, she felt a quick pleasure that he had survived. She'd been assuming, ever since the raid, that the Indian woman had killed him. "Do they still have you?"

"No," Andrew laughed raggedly. "They let me go. The Renegade insisted that the Indian put me right back where she found me."

"You're at the warehouse?"

"I was, but I'm not now. I'm not going to tell you where I am right now," Andrew said. "I'm not coming back."

Dizziness touched Claudia. "What do you mean, you're not –" She halted mid-sentence. She didn't want Klaus to realize what Andrew had just said.

Klaus, sitting beside her, staring down the long freeway as though facing an enemy, glanced over at her. "Tell him to meet us at the Anaheim office."

Claudia said, "Klaus wants you to meet us at the Anaheim office, Andrew."

There was a pause. "No. Tell him I'm sorry. I am sorry. But I'm not coming back."

Claudia held the phone away from her ear. She said to Klaus, "He says he can't. He —"

"Hang up," said Klaus. "He's lying to you. Those bastards still have him."

Claudia hung up with relief. She didn't want to lie to Klaus, and she didn't want to tell him the truth, either. She didn't want to betray Andrew, despite the fact that he was betraying the Cause. She was afraid, once they had dealt with the Renegade, that Klaus would ask her to hunt Andrew down and kill him. She hadn't had much luck with the Renegade, none of them had, but Claudia knew she would find Andrew, and she knew she would kill him, if they told her to.

Claudia thought that out of eleven people who had come to this planet, two had deserted. It didn't bode well for the eventual return of her people. She suspected that most of them, when they got here, would join in with the local skinheads, but the best and the brightest, the ones who'd been vaguely dissatisfied all along, would not. They'd do what Adolph had done, what Andrew was doing.

They'd desert.

The worst part of it was, she understood. The regimented existence that had been tolerable in the tunnels would not be tolerated here, could not be tolerated here. There were reasons to run —

— and places to run to.

She glanced at Klaus. And the mud people she'd heard so much about were really no worse than Klaus — not as bad, in some ways. At least the Indian woman wasn't intimidated by a steering wheel. Klaus still hadn't learned to drive and Claudia figured it was even money somebody would kill him before he did.

Klaus spoke in a voice that was almost dreamy. "Brian Schulz, Werner Schmidt, and John Bosworth, all dead. Jessica Landers is dead. That fucking magician ran over Gunther." His voice was very soft. "And they've got Andrew. And what do we have to show for it? Tell me, Claudia, what do we have to show for it?"

Claudia glanced at him, not exactly afraid; she'd seen him in this mood before. She could handle him. "One snuffed musician, who, according to Grant, could not possibly have been Adolph Stiegler."

"We're fighting in their back yard," said Klaus. "It gives them certain advantages."

Claudia stared at him coldly and tried to control the impulse to sneer. "Yes, that's right. We are in their back yard. What a wonderful analysis, Klaus. You've got the situation perfectly. All we have to do is convince them to come back to Venus, all five billion of them, ten or fifteen at a time, and fight us there." She turned her gaze back to the road, anger apparent in the line of her jaw. "Then we'd surely win, wouldn't we?"

It got a rise out of him. "You're insubordinate, Claudia."

Claudia *did* sneer now. "Report me."

He turned back to stare at the road again. "I will."

Venus was on the other side of the sun; they would not even be in radio contact again for another two months. Klaus's immediate superiors were a hundred and forty million miles away, and not getting closer any time soon. Claudia found it hard to take Klaus's threat seriously. There were more important things to worry about.

"FORTY YEARS AGO, four hundred and seven people fled Earth in space ships," said Andrew Peak.

The reporter's skepticism was evident. "Uh-huh."

"We landed on Venus, and only three of our five rockets survived. Two of them imploded on landing. The atmosphere on Venus is very dense, you know. Crushing."

The reporter shook his head. "No, I didn't know that."

"We've been there ever since. We dug tunnels into the ground. We had working hydrogen fusion for power back in 1955; you people *still* haven't figured that one out. We'd sell it to you, though," Andrew assured him. "We're not bad people, you see. We just need to leave Venus. Forty years ago, no one had a real concept of what Venus was like. We thought we'd be landing on a jungle planet. We thought we could survive there; we thought we could prosper." Andrew shook his head. "But we haven't prospered. We've barely replaced ourselves. We work eighteen and twenty hour days just to survive. We lose people in mining accidents all the time; we've lost dozens just getting the metals to build the rockets that are supposed to bring us back to Earth."

The interviewer leaned forward, propping his chin on his hand. "You know," he said, "you tell this story to the American government, and I bet you they'd whip on up there, gather up all you Venusians, bring the bunch of you back here, and then leave a bunch of NASA people behind. We could use a good base off of Earth, especially one that's already had forty years of work put into it. And with steady shipments of essentials, I bet you that place would thrive."

"Yes," said Andrew eagerly. "That's exactly correct. What we're suffering from, more than anything else, is a manpower problem. If –" He slowed down, and then stopped. The technicians behind the camera were snickering as he spoke.

The reporter said, "You got any monsters up there, Venusian monsters?"

Andrew said uncertainly, "No. Not as far as we know, anyway; nobody's ever gotten more than a couple dozen miles away from where we crash landed back in '55. There might be some elsewhere, but as long as we've been there, we've never seen anything living."

More snickering from behind the cameras, and now Andrew could see that even the interviewer was trying to keep a straight face. The man didn't believe him, didn't believe a word he'd said. "You're not going to run this, are you?" he asked quietly.

The reporter from *Hard Copy* said, "Oh, we'll run it."

MITCH WEBER AND Jeff Stone were waiting for them at the hotel room. That's all that was left; just the four of them. Klaus called ahead just before they reached the hotel, and Jeff, unobtrusively but heavily armed, met them down in the lobby as they arrived; he looked almost as pale and drawn as Claudia felt, and Claudia felt a brief flash of resentment; nobody had shot *him*. Then she remembered the old lady rapping him with that heavy black stick, and suddenly felt an irrational compassion for Jeff; being shot somehow didn't seem so bad, by comparison.

She brushed by Jeff as Klaus started explaining the debacle, the assault on the skinhead compound in Fontana . . . three hours ago. It seemed impossible to Claudia that it had only been three hours ago. She wanted a shower. She wanted to sleep for a year.

She wanted something, anything, to stop the throbbing in her arm. She slapped the palm of her hand against the elevator button. The door slid open instantly; she stepped inside, and turned around, holding the elevator door open with one hand for Klaus and Jeff.

Klaus and Jeff were nowhere near her. They were at the far end of the lobby, walking toward her . . . which was impossible. They'd only been a step or two behind her, the entire way, she had heard them walking behind her, Klaus talking at high speed –

She shook her head and when her eyes refocused on the lobby Dreadful Sam strode toward her, looking like Death itself. Smiling at her. She remembered his promise to kill her, remembered that she had not doubted him when he said it. She did not doubt him now. The hand holding the elevator door slipped free, and the elevator doors began to shut.

A hand shot out, catching them.

Claudia staggered backward, slamming against the far wall.

"Christ, Claudia," Jeff complained. "You couldn't wait ten seconds for us?"

Dreadful Sam was nowhere to be seen.

The elevator doors slid shut on the three of them; Claudia leaned back against the wall of the elevator, drained of strength, closing her eyes and waiting in the darkness for the elevator to reach the seventh floor, or for Dreadful Sam to kill her, whichever came first.

The doors opened on the seventh floor of the Disneyland Hotel, and Klaus and Jeff left her there in the elevator without waiting to see if she was following them.

Walkin' Talkin' Dave

THEY TOOK ALL the tables that had been scattered casually across the club area and moved them together to create a huge surface. Terminal Sue and Alec Armstrong spread out the documents she'd taken from the Nazi warehouse. Virtually all of them were in German – unfortunately, as Bogie had said once before, not a language they spoke. Alec Armstrong *did* speak it. He spoke it, read it, wrote it, and Sue suspected, thought in it. The man, in his passion for Nazi hunting, had become a reflection of what he sought – a real American hero, indeed.

"Much of this," Armstrong said, "is paperwork relating to the purchase of real estate."

"They're in Los Angeles," Terminal Sue protested. "They're buying the stuff from Americans. Wouldn't papers pertaining to things like that be in English?"

Armstrong shrugged. "If their native language is German, their internal paper work is going to be in German. Here, this is interesting. This whole stack here looks to be potential blackmail material. This might be quite useful –"

"Blackmail material regarding whom?" Blue Hair asked. Bogie knew that Blue Hair was eminently blackmailable, by people who had all the facts. Not that he and Dave could blackmail her, of course – they were guilty of all the same crimes.

Armstrong said, "The Fontana neo-Nazis, apparently."

"The only thing I like less than a neo-Nazi from Fontana is a Space Nazi from Hell," sneered Bogie Freedom.

"Anything on other locations?" Terminal Sue asked.

Bogie looked at her suspiciously. "Why do we care where their other locations are? We've got Blue Hair back; I don't want to have anything else to do with these people. Tomorrow's Friday. I have to deal with bands, with customers, with *metalheads*, in less than twenty hours. I'm not going to any other damn locations."

"Of course you are, Mr. Freedom. These people know where I live. They know where all of us live. They know where most of us work. This is an intolerable situation and it *must* be rectified." Blue Hair eyed Bogie. "We shall ignore, for the moment, your failure to open tonight. And as Ms. Walks-Far has stanched your bleeding, I see no reason you cannot be of service in dealing with the remainder of these hooligans."

Bogie protested. "I'm just an Entertainment Director. I'm not, not, not qualified to do this kind of work."

Blue Hair smiled at him and Bogie shivered. "I shall see that you have a very nice funeral, Mr. Freedom. The best that money can buy. A plot near my husband's . . . not too close, of course."

"Even if we destroy the Space Nazis," Bogie said, "we've still got neo-Nazis in Fontana. There are probably hundreds, if not thousands of them. Fontana is a big town."

Blue Hair shook her head. "Prior to the arrival of these Space Nazis, Mr. Freedom, this establishment never had a Nazi problem. Once the Space Nazis have been taken care of, I trust that matters will return to normal."

Terminal Sue smiled. She liked the way Blue Hair was discussing the Space Nazis as if they were vermin. Unfortunately, Terminal Sue was the only exterminator. She knew very well that Doctor Death had only shot people's clothing; the woman was a complete hypocrite who had probably never killed anyone in her life, and Terminal Sue had been glad to see her and her accomplice leave with Walkin' Talkin' Dave.

"Matters will *never* return to normal," Bogie said in despair. "They think I'm their damn renegade and Venus is full of Space Nazis. They'll just keep coming and coming and coming. They'll harass us until we all die."

Alec Armstrong shook his head. "I do not believe that there are that many of them on the planet at this point. Two ships are all that

I'm aware of; one person in the first ship, and ten in the second. A total of eleven."

"And that's another thing," said Bogie. "That renegade Nazi must be around here somewhere. If we could find him, then the Nazis could kill him and they could *stop* trying to kill me."

"I am afraid," said Blue Hair, "that that is not a viable solution, Mr. Freedom. I can no more allow the Space Nazis to kill their renegade than I can allow them to kill you."

Bogie stared at her. "You know who the renegade is?"

Blue Hair nodded, and said, as though it were the most obvious thing in the world, "Mr. Bradden, of course."

"Walkin' Talkin' Dave? Walkin' Talkin' Dave is the Nazi?" Terminal Sue's voice rose perilously. "But I thought it was Bogie."

"People on Venus," Bogie explained, "don't name their children 'Bogie Freedom.' Only hippies in Santa Barbara do that."

"That's your real name?" Terminal Sue stared at him. "I thought that was an alias. Who the hell would name a kid Bogie Freedom?"

"My sainted mother," said Bogie smugly. "She loved me."

TERMINAL SUE KICKED the door to the bedroom in.

Doctor Death said, "Hey." Kathy and Dave didn't even look up.

Terminal Sue stared in disbelief. She turned around, walked out of the bedroom and into the living room where Bogie Freedom was waiting. She jerked her thumb toward the bedroom. *"You* go get him."

Bogie disappeared into the bedroom.

Terminal Sue gave them enough time to get dressed, if they were so inclined, and then went in. She grabbed Bogie by his pony tail, kicked Dave on his naked ass, knocking him out of the swing and onto the floor, pointed one mean finger at Doctor Death and Kathy, and said, "Get dressed. *Now*."

Kathy pointed at the men. "They have to get dressed too, right?"

Terminal Sue said, "No, first I want to beat them. In places where the bruises won't show. And it'll hurt more if they're naked."

Doctor Death, kneeling on the trampoline, said, "Can we watch?"

IN THE CAR, with Bogie in the passenger seat of her Mustang, and Walkin' Talkin' Dave and the women in back, Terminal Sue said to Bogie Freedom, "I can't trust you, can I? I can't trust the damn Nazi, I understood that, but I thought I could at least trust you, when the situation is urgent, to *behave* as though it were urgent."

Bogie whined, "What did I do?"

"I am not," said Terminal Sue, "going to describe it." She tried to think of something to say that would hurt him, and couldn't –

It came to her.

"When we get back to the club," she said viciously, "go look at the game."

Bogie stared at her.

THE LAST EIGHT entries said *TS*.

The second entry said *BF*.

The high score on *Space Nazis From Hell* said *BFD*.

"That bitch," Bogie swore.

"THERE IS ONLY one question," said Blue Hair, "that is relevant at this point, Mr. Bradden." She paused. "I presume you wish to be *called* Mr. Bradden?"

Walkin' Talkin' Dave said, "Yes, ma'am."

Bogie said, "Call him Mr. Stiegler."

Dave couldn't contain himself. "How did you *know?*"

Blue Hair fixed an icy eye on him. The bad one. "I read your mail, Mr. Bradden, as it comes in. I read your mail from Nintendo. I read your mail *to* Nintendo."

Bogie said, "That's illegal."

Dave said doubtfully, "You read my mail *to* Nintendo?" She really *was* omniscient.

Blue Hair said, "And I quote, 'Goddamn bloodsucking corporate vampire Super-Mario-Brothers-obsessed no-taste Yellow Peril bastards.' In the future, Mr. Bradden, when a business negotiation has concluded unsatisfactorily, may I recommend a simple, 'Thank you for your consideration'?"

"But that's a good game," Dave protested.

Bogie and Sue both turned on him.

"You *wrote* that?" Terminal Sue said. She thought only an ex-Nazi would use the phrase "Yellow Peril."

"You write computer games?" Bogie asked. He wondered what else Dave was keeping from him. After all, Dave had never told him about the sunglasses; some doctor had had to tell him about that.

Dave looked at Bogie with a glint in his eye. "It's what I do," he said, "when I'm not doing other things."

Bogie was too excited to notice the blatant theft, even when Terminal Sue laughed out loud. "But I played that game for *years* and —"

"Hair dye and plastic surgery?" Terminal Sue asked.

"And a deep body tan, cowboy boots and a hat." Dave smiled modestly. "I've also bulked up quite a bit. I do a lot of free weight work — I use the Joe Wieder system. Tall, dark, and handsome, that's me." He grinned. "Bogie's the only scrawny, blond, Nazi-lookin' dude around here."

"That will be enough," said Blue Hair. "To the business at hand: Mr. Bradden, where *are* your erstwhile companions?"

"I don't know. I haven't talked to any of them in half a decade. When the first one showed up here, trying to kill Bogie, I didn't even know who it was. I thought maybe it had to do with that land deal –"

Blue Hair said sharply, "That will be quite enough on *that* subject. We are discussing the Space Nazis. Your erstwhile companions, Mr. Bradden. I must presume you have more of an insight into their behavior than the rest of us."

"They're probably in Orange County somewhere," said Dave. "That's just a guess. But they'd like it behind the Orange Curtain. It's clean, it's white except for the Vietnamese, and they'd just avoid those parts. I doubt they could find anywhere in Los Angeles that they'd feel comfortable."

"I bet they're at Disneyland," said Bogie.

Everyone looked at him.

Bogie shrugged. "If I was a Nazi and I'd been raised on Venus, I'd want to go to Disneyland."

Alec Armstrong looked up from the papers, and said, "I've got a telephone number here for the Disneyland Hotel, with a notation underneath it saying Room 702."

"I suggest," said Blue Hair, "that everyone get some sleep. You'll go in the morning."

Walkin' Talkin' Dave, who had been raised on Venus, smiled a huge, brilliant smile. "All right! I've never been to Disneyland," he told them.

Ramboing at the Disneyland Hotel

ON FRIDAY MORNING, in Walkin' Talkin' Dave's VW van, with the Deadhead stickers and peace signs in the back window and two surf boards, still in their bags, strapped to the roof, Bogie Freedom, Dave, Terminal Sue, Doctor Death and Kathy drove down the 5 freeway, south toward Orange County. It was half an hour after dawn, a time only Terminal Sue was familiar with.

Kathy held a hand up in front of her eyes and said, "What's the matter with the light?"

Bogie, who was seeing it for the second time in two days and the third time that week, said knowledgeably, "It's the morning."

Kathy looked unconvinced. "Oh."

Terminal Sue sat in the passenger's seat with her eyes closed. She felt like a fool. She suspected she was being a fool. Armstrong had vanished during the night, after agreeing to take part in today's raid. Today's Ramboing, as Bogie kept calling it. She suspected that only fools Ramboed.

She didn't blame Armstrong and wished that she'd had the good sense to do the same herself. She could have been in Anaheim hours ago.

She sat with her eyes closed as the van tooled down the freeway, trying to ignore the sounds coming from the back.

"The weather started getting rough, the tiny ship was tossed, if not for the courage of the fearless crew, the Minnow would be lost, the Minnow would be lost...."

When the song concluded, Dave said, as though it were the most important question in the world, "Do you think the Professor was doing mushrooms? I bet there were mushrooms all over that island."

Doctor Death said doubtfully, "He always kind of struck me as the Just Say No type."

"I think he was eating mushrooms," said Kathy. "He had a glazed look in his eyes."

"Ginger was doing Mary-Ann," said Dave. He'd grown up on Venus, sure, but he got Nick at Nite. He not only knew the theme song to *Gilligan's Island,* he knew the words to the *Brady Bunch* song too, and had the traditional crush on Marsha Brady.

Bogie added wistfully, "I would have done Mary-Ann."

Terminal Sue thought, *We're all going to get killed.* She straightened up, glancing around at the motley crew. They were a hairy bunch, she thought. Her own hair hung past her shoulders, but it was shorter than everyone else's, and perfectly straight; it stayed in place. The rest of the hair in the van went in several directions at once, even Bogie's, even with the pony tail. Terminal Sue supposed that was why he wore the hat, to keep his hair from sticking out all over. Having seen him once without his hat, it struck her as a good idea. And the hair spray. The amount of hair spray in the van could probably qualify it for an environmental disaster. How could she Rambo with people who used this much hair spray?

She looked Doctor Death in the eye and said, "You will shoot somebody today, won't you?"

Doctor Death nodded, looking at Terminal Sue sincerely. "Of course," she said. "I'll shoot lots of people."

Terminal Sue sagged back into her seat, closing her eyes again. It was going to be a long day, and God only knew how many people would have damaged clothing by the end of it.

MITCH WEBER, THEIR communications man and their pilot, sat at the console in their hotel room. He was patched into the microwave dish atop the hotel, and was beaming from there to a specially leased dish in an antenna farm several miles away; that dish was locked on the ship, in geosynchronous orbit above the Earth.

Claudia said furiously, "This is goddamn bonehead decision, you gutless son of a bitch."

Mitch and Jeff sat by silently as Klaus and Claudia fought. Neither of them wanted to get into the line of fire, either metaphorically or for real.

Klaus said, "File a protest when we get back. Until then, I'm in charge, and we *are* going back."

"You're a fucking idiot, and a coward, you're a fucking *coward,* Klaus! This is going to blow everything. We might, *might,* get the ship down without the American government tracking it. We'll *never* get it back up again without them knowing. You're blowing the mission, you're blowing the element of surprise, and *none* of it's necessary!" She was shouting by the time she got done, standing face to face with Klaus, glaring into his eyes.

Klaus's fury matched her own, and his voice was even louder. "This mission has been an unmitigated disaster from the very first. I no longer give a shit about the goddamn Renegade. Let him rot down here with the mud people. This mission has failed. They may shoot me for that when we get back, but we have to get back first. If we stay here we'll keep getting picked off one by one. We're outgunned and outnumbered and *they know we're here!*"

"They know we're on the planet!" Claudia shouted. "They know we're in Southern California! They don't know we're *here.*"

Machine gun fire tore through the door to their hotel room.

Claudia dove to the floor. Bullets sprayed the wall behind her, caught Mitch Weber and threw him back against the wall.

Jeff Stone, standing at the far side of the room, calmly, with one shot, blew Alec Armstrong's head off as the old man came in through the door he'd just ruined.

Weber staggered to his feet. "Son of a bitch broke my ribs," he gasped.

Claudia slowly got to her feet. "Give it a minute," she said contemptuously, glancing at the bullet-proof vest visible beneath his shirt. "You just had the wind knocked out of you."

Klaus stood over the dead old man, screaming hatred down at the motionless body, and started kicking him. Claudia watched Klaus lose it, Klaus screaming at the dead man at the top of his lungs, kicking him savagely, one kick after the other, kicking the body across the rug, across the room, until it fetched up against the wall. Klaus stood there kicking it as its arms and ribs cracked audibly, mixing English and German obscenities in a steady, unending stream.

Claudia looked away and found Jeff and Mitch looking at her.

"Evacuate," she said wearily. "We're going to have police here in minutes."

Mitch glanced at the control board. "We can't leave the equipment here. This panel has direct links to the control circuitry aboard the ship."

The sound of Klaus's voice, screaming, almost drowned out Mitch's words. Claudia glared at him with pure hatred, pulled her gun, and shot him in the back of the head.

The stream of obscenities stopped abruptly, and Klaus collapsed atop the old man's corpse. Claudia found the energy to wonder briefly who the old man had been, but it hardly mattered at this point. She gestured to the control panel. "Pick it up," she ordered.

The two men stared at her, unmoving.

"Right *now*," she yelled at them. She gave them the same glare she'd just directed at the back of Klaus's head; and Jeff and Mitch finally moved, each of them picking up one end of the control panel that was their only remaining link to the ship.

Claudia said, "Let's go."

TERMINAL SUE TOOK the stairs. She wasn't getting in any goddamn elevators, not when people were wandering around the hotel with guns. She'd just heard what sounded like machine gun fire, followed by at least two handguns being discharged; people got shot to death in elevators because they couldn't run and they couldn't hide.

Bogie Freedom followed her, refusing to let his wound prevent him from being at least as manly as Terminal Sue. They burst out of the stairwell, into the seventh floor lobby of the Disneyland Hotel.

It was quiet. Sue held a finger up to her lips, and then took the corridor off to the right; the sign mounted on the wall said, 700-724, with an arrow pointing off to the right. Room 702 was just around the corner; Terminal Sue followed her gun through the door, looking cautiously at the two bodies in the corner; she scouted through the connecting doorway into the adjoining suite, checking the closets and the bathroom. Empty –

She heard Bogie shout, "Space Nazis!"

THE CONTROL BOARD lay in the middle of the hallway.

Doctor Death looked it over when the elevator deposited them on the seventh floor. The Space Nazis were nowhere to be seen; neither were Bogie or Terminal Sue.

The board looked like something out of a good 1950s science fiction movie; bread-board electronics, elegantly put together; dials and gauges and levers and switches covered its surface. A tiny keypad sat over in one corner. Antennae jutted up from its back.

Its lights were dark. Doctor Death said to Dave, "What the hell is this? Should I shoot it?"

Dave squatted down to look at it. He looked back up at Doctor Death almost immediately. "It's a remote. We used them to pilot remotes on the surface of Venus, to send vehicles off to places where people couldn't go. I've never seen one quite like this, though." He glanced back down at it again, reading dials with German labels on them, and looked back up at Doctor Death again. "I think it's for their ship. The ship they must have come here in."

Kathy said, "Can you use it to send commands to the ship?"

Walkin' Talkin' Dave nodded slowly. "Probably. But it's going to take some time."

"Let's do it then," said Kathy definitely. "Let's make the ship crash."

Dave said flatly, "No. It's gotta be a big ship. It'll come down on somebody. It'll kill them."

"Drop it in the ocean," Doctor Death suggested.

"That'll cause a –" Dave stopped abruptly, a grin lighting up his face. "Okay," he agreed. "Into the ocean it is." He glanced around the corridor. "This is going to take a while. We better find somewhere to hide before the Disney police arrest us. Someplace with a plug."

BOGIE, WHO HAD surreptitiously taken pain killers in Walkin' Talkin' Dave's van, flew down the stairs after the Space Nazis. Terminal Sue ran after him. For someone who'd just been shot two days ago, Terminal Sue thought Bogie ran pretty good. She was having difficulty keeping up with him.

Bogie hollered, *"Woohoo!"* His painkillers were *good* painkillers.

The Nazis had dropped some big contraption in the corridor down the ways from their room when Terminal Sue and Bogie had started chasing them. They'd fled down the back stairs, and Terminal Sue hoped desperately that they hadn't decided to wait for them on one of the floors below, guns drawn, to shoot both Bogie and Terminal Sue as they rounded one of the corners.

It was what Terminal Sue would have done if somebody had tried to chase *her* down a flight of stairs. But then again, Bogie was moving so rapidly that he would just barrel into them, bowling them over, and then, thought Terminal Sue, she would have an opportunity to shoot them all.

Bogie shouted *"Woohoo!"*

Terminal Sue wondered what painkillers he was using. He was having way too much fun. She knew that Walkin' Talkin' Dave, Doctor Death, and Kathy were probably off having fun somewhere, too. Everyone except Terminal Sue and the Nazis were having fun.

Bogie leapt into the air, missed one flight of stairs entirely, moving from one landing to the next, and shouted again, *"Woohoo!"*

Terminal Sue paused at the top of the stairwell – and then leapt into the air, and followed him, flying down the flight, not touching a single stair. When she landed, she hollered, *"Woohoo!"*

It was not a noise she had ever made before.

They ran down the stairs, shouting *"Woohoo!"* together.

THE SPACE NAZIS reached the ground floor. For a moment, Claudia couldn't hear the maniacs hollering behind them. She knew that if the Renegade and the Indian caught them, they would murder them all; and they would have fun, and they would holler silly things while they did it.

She had heard them yelling *"Woohoo"* while running down the entire seven flights of stairs. She had heard the noise only once before, just before the pair of them and their friends had demolished the compound in Fontana; just moments after someone, probably the Indian woman, had shot her in the arm.

Their car was parked in the lot outside the hotel. Claudia sprinted for it and reached it before the men; she didn't intend to let either of them drive. She slid in behind the wheel of the Mercedes, fumbled with the keys and got them inserted as Jeff and Mitch scrambled into the back seat. They shot out their own back window and started firing at the exit they had just left through. Claudia, watching it happen in the rear view mirror, still didn't believe it; the Renegade burst through the door, shouted, *"Woohoo!"* and, without Jeff or Mitch even getting a shot off at him, fainted.

TERMINAL SUE BURST out of the stairway exit, seconds behind Bogie. She tripped over him, falling ungracefully, landing almost on her head and then rolling into the gutter. Bullets struck the wall behind them. Terminal Sue crawled back to Bogie; they'd shot the damn fool coming out the door, they'd done exactly what she'd been afraid they were going to do, and now Bogie was dead and it was her fault for not making him stay behind her.

As she reached him, Bogie's eyes fluttered open and he said, "Did we catch them?"

The Nazis car skidded out of the parking lot, heading away from them.

The only wound on his entire body was the hole in his shoulder. Terminal Sue stared at him indignantly; he hadn't even been shot. Sue scrambled to her feet, grabbing Bogie by his leather vest and began kicking him in areas that weren't too close to his shoulder wound. "Get up, get up!" she yelled at him. "They're getting away and you're lounging in the gutter!"

"I feel sick," Bogie said weakly.

"I'll tell Blue Hair, goddamn you! Get up, get up!"

Bogie lurched to his feet and they ran for the van.

They didn't reach it. There was an unguarded red '69 Malibu Chevelle convertible with the top down sitting in the parking lot near the exit the Nazis had taken. Bogie leapt onto it, skidded across the hood, and scrambled into the driver's seat. He started the engine faster than Terminal Sue could have done it with a key. Terminal Sue jumped into the passenger seat, looked at Bogie severely and said, "You better not faint while you're driving."

"I *never* faint while I'm driving," Bogie snarled.

They peeled out of the hotel parking lot, and went zooming after the Nazis.

Terminal Sue looked at him with something close to hate, and said, "Don't get me in any shade."

THE RENEGADE AND the Indian came after them in a red sports car with the top down. Claudia watched them in the rear view mirror, gaining on her. The Renegade was driving. As she watched, the Indian stood up in her seat, pointed a heavy semi-automatic at them, and began firing. The bullets ripped into the rear of the Mercedes, and Claudia swerved through the early morning rows of traffic, people arriving at Disneyland, blasted across the street separating the hotel from Disneyland and found herself heading toward the fence.

The fence was a huge wall of shrubbery, fifteen feet high, backed by a chain link fence. None of her options were good; Claudia aimed for the center of the fence and smashed through it at nearly sixty miles an hour, the heavy Mercedes exploding into Fantasyland.

Tourists screamed and scattered. People dressed in stupid outfits did nothing to calm them.

The Mercedes slewed around as Claudia hit the brakes, turning into a slide, moving *much* too fast: for just an instant they were moving sideways, heading down the cobblestone street at forty or fifty miles an hour with the car pointed at a perfect right angle, and then the car flipped, turned in mid-air and smashed into the side of a building.

The front end of the Mercedes splashed like water, folding up into a quarter the original space. Claudia threw herself down and to the side as the steering wheel smashed into the seat above her head and the engine's block came crashing up through the dashboard. The Mercedes literally bounced back off the wall and rolled one last time, the car going one way, the engine heading off in the other direction, and then came to a stop upside down.

The back seat doors opened.

Claudia said weakly, "Jeff? Mitch?"

Through the upside down windows she saw them both, saw their legs, from the knees down, staggering out of the car. One pair of legs stopped briefly just in front of her face –

She heard Mitch yell in German, "Come on, Jeff!"

They both ran away, into the crowds that had, just barely, stopped screaming.

Instants later, another pair of legs ran by the car. She heard the Indian woman yelling, "Jesus Christ, Bogie, I *know* you can run faster than *that!*"

Then there was silence again.

In the distance, she saw tourists staring at her, making no move to approach the car. A person wearing a Goofy costume took one hesitant step forward, then stood watching her.

With her right hand, Claudia reached above her head. She groped for the switch that would lower the window, and enable her to crawl out. She found one switch, toggled it. Nothing. She tried the switch next to it and the passenger's door lock snapped shut. She sagged back down against the roof of the car, trying to ignore the half dozen places that screamed in pain, and then shifted onto her side so she could get at her gun. It took her thirty seconds to worm the gun free one-handed, get it up over her head and fire it into the front passenger door's window.

The tourists screamed again.

She threw the gun out into Main Street, and with her one good hand ripped her blouse open, popping buttons, and then pushed herself through the broken window, out into the street. She rolled into a sitting position, looked around at the Japanese tourists and the tourists from Idaho, at the half dozen Disneyland security guards, all men, all young, approaching her with their guns drawn.

As they approached her, Claudia Hess said plaintively, "I need medical help, I'm bleeding, did you see what those men *did* to me?" She looked at the closest one, said beseechingly, "Please, call the police. Get me ... a doctor," she whispered as he got close enough for the whisper to be effective.

THE BLOOD-SPATTERED woman with the bandage on her arm fainted and slumped into a pool of her own blood as the security guards surrounded her.

Ass Over Teacup

JEFF GRABBED MITCH by the arm, dragging him almost to a stop. They were far enough from the wreck of the Mercedes that their running was only drawing attention to them. "Slow down," he panted. He swerved abruptly to the right, still holding Mitch by the arm, and moved into a small walkway between two rides. "Put your gun away," he told Mitch, and tucked his under his shirt, into his waistband. Out of the corner of his eye, he saw the Renegade and the Indian. He dragged Mitch around another corner, and immediately got into the shortest line around.

Mitch fought for breath. He thought that Claudia had been wrong, that the old bastard's bullets had broken his ribs. He winced every time he moved. "We've got to . . . get out of here."

"No we don't." Jeff reached over and wiped the sweat off Mitch's face with his own sleeve. "Disneyland is a big place, and there are thousands and thousands of people here. All we have to do is get lost and not let them find us. Try to look like you're having fun," he said.

DAVE CARRIED ONE end of the control panel, and Doctor Death and Kathy carried the other. Dave walked backward, because Doctor Death told him to. "Do you have any idea where you want to go with this?" Dave asked Doctor Death. "I thought we'd duck into one of the hotel rooms."

"No," said Doctor Death. "We have to go down to the fifth floor. I know a guy who lives there."

Dave looked doubtful. "You know someone who lives in the Disneyland Hotel?"

Doctor Death nodded. "Uh-huh. A tattooed dude."

"I don't know," Dave began, and then had to stop because their elevator had arrived, and Doctor Death and Kathy were pushing him into it.

Disneyland Hotel security officers erupted out of the second elevator moments after the first elevator's doors had closed on the three.

THE TATTOOED DUDE, Chad, sat in the middle of his room and watched Dave work the control panel. It was obvious that Chad had lived in that room for a long time; the walls were covered with posters of Disney characters. *Chad* was covered with Disney characters. Walkin' Talkin' Dave kept shooting covert looks at Chad, who was half undressed. Mickey and Minnie were doing something unsavory on his chest, while Goofy tooled along his stomach in an old jalopy, being chased by Pluto.

Kathy said, "I always liked Warner Brothers better."

Doctor Death nodded. "Bugs had attitude."

Chad looked offended. "I didn't *have* to let you guys use my plug." He glanced pointedly at his watch. "It's almost time for me to go to Disneyland."

Doctor Death knew that Chad went to Disneyland every day. He had bought *something* out of every single shop in the entire park, had ridden on every one of the rides. He existed on ice cream and candy and soda pop, and never threw up, not even on the most violent rides.

He'd been to every show in the park multiple times, and he still laughed at the bears over in Frontierland. Chad liked everything about the park. He liked the clean, youthful employees, he liked the invisible ones, hidden inside their Disneyland costumes. He *loved* the ghosts in the Haunted House. He knew them all by name, and had been carrying on a romance for years with one of the lady ghosts. He had fleetingly stalked the woman who played Alice in Wonderland; she was nothing like the kid in the book. Chad wasn't opposed to kids, but why stalk one? He'd stopped stalking Alice when she'd been replaced by a new woman whose legs weren't nearly as pretty.

"This won't take long," Kathy assured Chad. "You can trust us. We're your *friends*."

Chad looked skeptical. Doctor Death helped him.

Dave leaned over the control board. He had a piece of paper at his side and was writing down readings off the board. A couple of the gauges weren't labeled, but he thought he'd figured it out. He moved one dial slightly clockwise, flipped a lever, watching the gauge that showed, he thought, the level of fuel left for the rockets. The gauge flickered, the needle dropping a very small amount. He tapped numbers into the keypad, watching the gauges again . . . then said, "We have to wait about thirty seconds so I can be sure this is doing what I want it to. Then we can destroy it."

There was a sharp rap at the door.

Everyone froze. Kathy whispered to Chad, "Go answer the door and tell whoever it is to go away."

Chad yelled, "Help! Help!"

The door opened and an elderly Mexican woman stuck her head hesitantly inside. "E'scuse me?" She looked at Doctor Death and Kathy and Dave –

Chad yelled, "Help! Help!"

The old woman turned and fled.

Doctor Death whipped across the room, slammed the door, and locked it. She looked at Chad. "You'll be sorry for that."

There was another sharp rap.

Doctor Death taunted Chad. "I dare you. Scream for help."

Chad looked at her, then at Kathy, then at Walkin' Talkin' Dave. He looked back at Doctor Death.

He yelled, "Help! Help!"

A SWAT team burst through the door. "Everybody freeze!" the first officer in through the door yelled. All of them were in that crouch that cops were prone to assuming whenever they pulled their guns.

"I can't do that," said Chad reasonably. "I have to go to Disneyland."

Dave leaned forward and pressed a button. "There," he said, "that should do it." He eyed the board with complete satisfaction, and chortled. "If you wanna shoot something," he said to the SWAT guys, "you can shoot this board. I don't need it anymore."

One of them near the door twitched, but his commander glared at him and he restrained himself.

Doctor Death, who was a woman of action, picked up the far end of the control panel, heaved it in the general direction of the SWAT team, and dove for the floor. The other three hit the ground only instants after she did.

The SWAT team blew the control panel out of the air in an amazing display of coordinated firepower. It reached the ground in several distinct chunks.

The SWAT cops all grinned at each other. "That's what we get paid the big bucks for," one of them said proudly.

The boss SWAT cop waved his gun casually at the occupants of the room, and said, "You're all under arrest."

"TRY TO LOOK like you're having fun," said Bogie. "You're drawing attention to us."

"I *am* having fun," snapped Terminal Sue, which would have been true a week ago. But all this chasing and being chased and shooting at and being shot at was starting to wear on her. She thought sullenly that she'd had fun running down the stairs, and it dawned on her suddenly that Bogie had *also* had fun running down the stairs, and that it was the kind of thing that would have entertained Doctor Death, and Kathy, and Walkin' Talkin' Dave. She was associating, she thought, far too much with the wrong sort of people, the sort Blue Hair would have called the "wrong element."

The interesting thought struck her, just as suddenly, that Blue Hair had surrounded herself with a *lot* of the wrong element, and surely it wasn't an accident –

"Hey," said Bogie, "want to go on *Mister Toad's Wild Ride?* I love *Mister Toad's Wild Ride.* We gotta track down Dave and take him on that ride. He's never been to Disneyland," he told Terminal Sue sincerely.

"We have to catch the bad guys first," Terminal Sue said stubbornly. Even if she planned on associating with the wrong element, even if she planned on using words like "woohoo" in the future, she was still the best detective in Los Angeles. So she hadn't known that Dave was the renegade Nazi. Everybody was entitled to one mistake. "Bad guys first," she said out loud. *"Mister Toad's Wild Ride* second."

"It's a Small World third," Bogie said.

Terminal Sue looked at him in despair. Everyone else she'd ever met hated the *It's a Small World* ride. It figured Bogie would like it. Doctor Death and Kathy and Walkin' Talkin' Dave probably liked *It's a Small World,* too; Doctor Death and Kathy had probably had sex on that ride, with all the little dolls watching. "I refuse to sit in any of those little boats that Doctor Death and Kathy have been in before," Terminal Sue said finally.

Bogie nodded in understanding.

Terminal Sue scanned the crowds as they walked along. There were a lot of security guards around, doing the same thing. She was looking for two tall blond men; Claudia, trapped in the car, had certainly been taken into custody by security, and from what Terminal Sue had seen of her as they ran by, the woman was in no shape to cause anyone any further trouble. She calculated: from the ten Nazis who had arrived on the second ship, there were only four left alive, and that was counting Andrew Peak. Claudia was in custody, Klaus dead in the Disneyland Hotel, and Terminal Sue thought with a sudden fierce longing that if they could just capture or kill the remaining two Nazis, she could go to the beach. For a month.

Without Bogie.

"If I was a Nazi," said Bogie craftily, watching Terminal Sue to see how it was going over, "I'd go on *Mister Toad's Wild Ride.*"

"Oh, would you?" Terminal Sue asked, her eyes continuing to wander through the crowd. There, over on the left, there were a good dozen tall young blond men, but they were too young, were wearing bright Hawaiian shorts and talking in an accent that had more to do with the Sherman Oaks Galleria than with Space Nazis from Hell. Terminal Sue thought wistfully back to the days when she would have shot at one of them just for the hell of it. Teenage blond dudes, after all, might grow up to be adult blond dudes like Bogie. Or Carlo van Zandt, or the Space Nazis, or the neo-Nazis skinheads. Yes, she concluded, the world would be a better place if all the blond dudes were done away with.

She spotted two tall blond men in the line for the teacup ride. "There," she nudged Bogie, "the guys in the teacup line." All she could see was the back of their heads, but they were the right height, they were both blond, and one of them was wearing a red baseball cap that might have been Jeff Stone's Chicago Bulls cap. And how many grown men, after all, went to Disneyland together?

"It looks like them," Bogie agreed doubtfully. One of the men was holding the other one by the elbow. "Either that, or they're gay."

Terminal Sue changed course to head for the teacup line. As she did so the line started moving. The two blond men passed through the gate, one tugging the other forward onto the multi-colored platform, and they slid into a green and blue teacup. Terminal Sue ran forward, shoved two young children out of the way, and confronted the ride operator.

"I have to go on this ride."

Bogie trotted up behind her. "Me too," he agreed.

The two blond men had just about settled down in their tea cup. Terminal Sue still couldn't see their faces. "I have to go talk to two of the riders out there," Terminal Sue told the attendant.

The extremely young attendant shook his head. Before speaking to them, he turned his head and spat out a piece of chewing gum. "These other people were here before you. I can't allow you to take cuts. You don't have any right to be jumping in line on people."

"I don't," Terminal Sue agreed. "But I do have a gun."

"Are you going to kill somebody?"

Terminal Sue glanced at the back of the blond men's heads. "I might."

The boy shook his head. "I can't let you go in there and kill people. Uncle Walt wouldn't have liked that."

"I could stay out here and kill you," Terminal Sue offered.

The boy continued to shake his head; Disneyland had extremely loyal employees. "You can't take cuts."

Bogie, who knew all about harsh employers, said, "If you don't let us in, I'll tell your bosses that you were rude to us. And that you littered."

The ride started up, the platform slowly beginning to spin.

In despair, the boy glanced over at the offending piece of gum. The blond guy had him. They'd fire him for littering. He jerked his thumb at the ride. "You're in."

The platform was moving now at some speed. The two men in the green and blue teacup sat back on the bench, neither of them touching the wheel at the teacup's center. "Damn," said Bogie in disbelief. "Look at that. Neither of them are going to spin." He shook his head. "They won't get a very good ride that way."

Terminal Sue jumped onto the spinning platform. She came down hard, grabbed with her left hand at the nearest thing available to stabilize herself. It was one of the teacups, which was spinning in a direction opposite that of the spinning platform. She staggered, almost falling, and then Bogie leapt nimbly onto the platform. Bogie, who had learned from her mistakes, didn't try to use anything except Terminal Sue to keep his balance. He put one hand on her back as she was trying to keep her feet, knocking her down to the spinning platform.

Terminal Sue rolled over on her back and glared up at Bogie. "Get the hell away from me."

Bogie wasn't even looking at her. He stared across the length of the platform, at an unoccupied pink teacup. It had been intended for the children that Terminal Sue had cut off. If they were going to be on the ride, he thought, they might as well have a teacup.

One of the blond dudes shouted something at Bogie in German. Bogie glanced at the blond dude, and then down at Terminal Sue. "If they're not really the Nazis," he suggested, "we should grab that pink teacup."

Terminal Sue grabbed his vest. She used it to haul herself to her feet, then shoved Bogie away from her, and pulled her Ruger from its holster beneath her coat. Everybody was busy spinning and nobody even noticed the gun, except the two Nazis. She moved forward, through the spinning teacups toward the non-spinning teacup, bringing the BlackHawk up to point at them.

Jeff Stone stood up in the teacup.

Terminal Sue sighted down the length of the barrel at him. She felt herself beginning to smile, and thought to herself that she was spending way, way, way too much time with Bogie.

The man reached inside his sports coat.

Terminal Sue shot him three times.

The first shot blew a hole in his coat, the second shot blew the hideaway holster off his belt, and the last shot blew the Chicago Bulls cap off his head, sent it flying up into the air as though the man had tossed it. Jeff Stone slowly raised his hands above his head. The other Nazi, sitting next to him, didn't even stand up; he just put his hands on top of his head and closed his eyes.

When she'd been in the living room with Andrew Peak, she'd heard Bogie saying that he would be going to Heaven, and had heard Dreadful Sam say that *she,* Terminal Sue, might end up in Hell.

Fuck *that*. If Bogie Freedom deserved to go to Heaven, Terminal Sue thought *she* certainly deserved to go to Heaven.

Terminal Sue wanted to shoot Jeff again, twice, in the shoes, but the other teacup riders had started screaming after the first three shots. She took her eyes off Jeff long enough to see what had happened to Bogie –

He was in the pink teacup, spinning madly.

"THAT WAS GOOD shooting," Bogie said admiringly. He thought that he could learn to shoot like that, if his hands weren't cuffed behind his back.

The Disneyland cop said politely, "Shut up."

Bogie, who had been threatened by Blue Hair, ignored the man. "How much do you suppose our bail is going to be?" he asked Terminal Sue. "Blue Hair won't bail me out if it's too much. Sometimes she doesn't bail me out just to teach me a lesson."

Terminal Sue, sitting on the bench next to Bogie, hands cuffed behind her back, said, "I'll call my lawyer. He'll come and get us out. They don't have anything on us. I have a carry permit for the gun, and these guys smashed through the fence to break into Disneyland. We were just being good citizens chasing them."

Bogie looked doubtful. "We snuck into Disneyland. How much time can you get for something like that?"

"Community service," said Terminal Sue.

"Damn," said Bogie. He was sick of community service.

She eyed the Nazis, who were sitting on the bench beside them. "And once we're bailed out, then we'll lurk outside the courthouse and wait for the Nazis to come out. And *then* we'll get them." She didn't think she'd ever used the word *lurk* before. It was a good word.

"Lurk," Bogie said happily. It was a word he would have used.

The Happiest Place On Earth

WHILE TERMINAL SUE was busy shooting holes in Jeff Stone's clothing, the senior security officer on duty was trying to find out how badly Claudia Hess was injured.

She was not conscious; the doctor had an I.V. inserted into her arm, and was wiping the blood off her with alcohol swabs. "Hard to say," the doctor said. "I'm not sure how much blood she's lost; her heartbeat is quite strong." The doctor glanced up at the security guard. He nodded toward Claudia's bandaged arm. "There's a bullet wound under that bandage," he said.

The security officer, who was a touch older than all the fresh-faced young men who had brought Claudia to the first aid station, looked gravely concerned. "We've got some real bad guys here. I've got men throughout the park looking for them, and I've alerted the Anaheim police. If that woman wakes up, I want to talk to her."

Claudia's eyes fluttered, but didn't open. She'd heard every word the men had said. She waited until the security officer left the room, and when the doctor leaned over her again, reached up for him with her good right hand, and grabbed the man's stethoscope.

WHEN THE SECURITY officer came back, not five minutes later, the patient was gone, and the doctor lay half naked on the cold, un-carpeted floor, with his own stethoscope wrapped tightly around his neck.

CLEAN, WEARING THE doctor's shirt, her hair loose and partially hiding the cuts on her forehead, Claudia Hess wandered casually into the park. The first thing she did was buy an ice cream bar for camouflage.

She walked down Main Street, eating her ice cream bar. Security personnel were all over the place, watching the crowds, stopping people and asking them questions. Claudia stopped at one of the little shops that lined Main Street and browsed through the toys and hats and t-shirts while a pair of security guards passed by outside. She bought herself a little visor that kept the sun out of her eyes, and had a map of Disneyland on it.

She had to kill time. Except for the doctor, nobody had gotten a really good look at her face when blood was not streaming down it from the cut on her forehead. She thought she might be able to get out, later in the afternoon, possibly with someone else's baby as further camouflage. Ice cream and babies, she thought.

She timed the groups of security guards, watching them sweep back and forth across Main Street, USA; as the second batch passed by the little shop, she stepped out behind them and headed north on Main Street. A group of tourists, about a dozen white people from some vowel state, were making their slow way up Main Street and Claudia attached herself to them, walking as close by them as she could without making the tourists aware of her.

The tourists weren't in a hurry; Claudia listened to the snatches of their conversation that she could make out. They were going to Frontierland, to take the Mark Twain riverboat over to Treasure Island.

It was a long walk to Frontierland. The path curved off toward the left, and Claudia found herself relaxing slightly. Most of the crowd seemed to have no idea that anything was wrong elsewhere in the park. Aside from the excess of security guards it was a gorgeous summer day. Warm, with a faint breeze, the sun wearing down on her, relaxing her, pushing the tension out of her –

The adrenaline rush she'd been riding collapsed all at once. Claudia took another step, and then found herself standing motionless, watching the tourists moving away from her, without the energy to keep following them. She forced herself to take another step, and it was the hardest thing she'd ever done in her life, fighting the lethal wave of fatigue; if she blew it now they'd have her within minutes, and she knew they wouldn't make the mistake of leaving her alone with a civilian again. Another step, and another, and she was walking again, pushing forward through the warm, syrupy air, half a dozen steps behind the tourists the security officers were supposed to think she was with.

The cobblestone path wound around on a long, gentle arc. Benches lined the path, and the temptation to go sit down on one of them was almost irresistible. Claudia fought it, fought to keep from stumbling as she moved forward, unconnected thoughts buzzed through her mind, swarming. God, she felt tired. The last time she'd felt this tired was – good Lord, a *long* time ago; she hadn't been this tired since Sam had killed her. She hadn't slept in the four days before her death, for wondering when Sam was going to come for her; the wizard was deceitful, a lying bastard who knew almost as much as she did, and didn't love her, and couldn't be trusted.

Behind her, the security guard said politely, "Ma'am?"

The voice came from a great distance away. Claudia ignored it, kept moving forward, and the guard said, in a deeper voice this time, "Look at me."

He was standing there when she turned, wearing the guard's uniform, wearing the guard's body, looking at her out of the guard's eyes. Where a gun should have been, a knife hung. A long, wicked, bright silver knife.

The knife –

– rising, rising, the young wizard's gray eyes glowing red with heat as he brought the glowing knife up above his head and brought it down. Through the immense shock of pain she saw it, her blood covering his arms to the elbows, the knife glowing like the moon –

"You *did* kill me."

"Yes."

She backed away from him, from the security guard, from a tall man with dead gray eyes, backing one step and then two, and oh, God, she remembered it, the wizard wasn't crazy and neither was she, because she remembered her own death, the arc of the knife coming down on her –

Claudia Hess, whom Dreadful Sam had loved in a different time, ran for her life through the Happiest Place on Earth.

SHE FOUND A bathroom and hid in it. Half a dozen adult women and three or four small girls were using it when she ducked inside, panting for breath; Claudia gasped, "I'm so sorry, I think I'm going to throw up," and got herself inside the one empty stall before she did.

She kneeled, hunched over the toilet, shivering, once the spasms had stopped and her stomach was empty of the ice cream bar; the ice cream bar was all that was in it, was the only thing she'd eaten since yesterday afternoon, eighteen hours ago. She flushed it and put down the lid, and then sat back on it, head resting against the tile wall behind her, trying to catch her breath, when reality blurred around her.

He stood in the middle of Main Street, motionless, waiting, a man dressed in darkness, dressed in mourning. The ancient silver knife, the knife that had been forged before Christ had been born, hung at his belt, tucked incongruously through one of the loops. People saw him but did not notice him, not even those who had to alter their paths to walk around him. He stood with his back to the park's exit; waiting for her to come to him. The blackness about him was absolute, a lack of color and of sharpness that was as much the work of Dreadful Sam's soul as his magic, if those two things were not after all the same thing –

It came to her what she would say to him, what she had been waiting to say to him for so long.

Reality settled back into place.

Everything settled into place.

Claudia Hess sat on the lid of the toilet, in a bathroom that had grown suddenly silent, staring sightlessly. For the first time in a life that had never made sense, it *did* make sense. The tunnels she had been born in and the long journey she had made, from one world to another, to oceans and the smell of salt and the feel of Dreadful Sam body pressing her down into the bed: the rage and the pain and all the deaths. All of it had led to this moment, to the man who was waiting for her.

The door to the bathroom opened without her touching it.

A security guard stood there looking down at her. Claudia met his eyes and they didn't belong to Dreadful Sam.

Claudia stood and brushed by him, let him live; walked through the guards clustered at the entrance to the woman's bathroom, untouched and unseen. She had the strength left to do this last thing; it was enough. The sunlight that had threatened to overwhelm her moments before did not touch her; the gentle breeze moved across skin that belonged to someone else. Claudia walked perfectly erect, head back, through the crowds of tourists, and onto Main Street.

Dreadful Sam pulled the knife free as she approached; Claudia stopped five feet away from him, and smiled at him with a smile that belonged to a woman long dead. "Come here, Sam."

He moved forward in a wall of encroaching blackness that shut out the Sun.

THE SECURITY GUARDS arrived en masse, not long after the first scream. One of them threw up at the sight of the woman's corpse. Another, with more presence of mind, began working the crowd, trying to find someone who had seen the crime, who had seen anything.

One young Mexican girl, twelve years old, said that she had seen *el Diablo* kill the blond woman and then walk away.

Red Is The Rose, Red Is Redemption

THEY SPENT THE night in the jail.

Walkin' Talkin' Dave snored. It was an amazing sound. Terminal Sue, Doctor Death and Kathy were all imprisoned in the cell next to Bogie and Dave and Chad; they could talk to each other, but couldn't see each other. The justice system hadn't gotten around to remanding them all to the county jails, where they would have been segregated by sex.

"Man," said Bogie, "I hope Blue Hair bails us out in the morning."

Terminal Sue said, "Don't hold your breath. You have to have charges filed against you before you can make bail. It's going to take a while for my lawyer to reach a judge." She paused. "It's a good thing we all got arrested before Claudia got killed, or we'd never make bail."

Bogie nodded. The police had questioned them all about it; somebody had stabbed Claudia and left her in the middle of Main Street. Fortunately everybody had been arrested already when it happened. "I always see a judge the next morning," Bogie said. "That way I get bailed out right away."

There was a pause in Walkin' Talkin' Dave's snoring. Dave said in a gravelly, sleep-infested voice, "Unless Blue Hair wants to teach us a lesson."

Bogie could hear the skepticism in Terminal Sue's voice. "Blue Hair gets you to a judge first thing in the morning when you get arrested? I have one of the best lawyers in Los Angeles, and even he sometimes doesn't get me out until noon."

Bogie shook his head. "Blue Hair always has us see a judge in the morning."

Terminal Sue said with curiosity, "How often do you get arrested, anyway?"

"Rarely," said Bogie instantly.

"Hardly ever," Dave's sleepy voice agreed.

Doctor Death said smugly, "I've never been arrested before."

Kathy didn't say anything.

Chad, curled up on his bunk, curled up into an even tighter ball, refusing to participate in this conversation.

Bogie said, "Kathy?"

There was a long silence. Then Kathy said, "I don't think they should be able to arrest you for some things. Moral crimes aren't the same as actively breaking the law, I mean, when there's no *victim*. You know? Doesn't that seem unfair to you? It seems unfair to me," she said conclusively.

Terminal Sue lay in her bunk and stared at both Kathy and Doctor Death. "Do moral crimes," she wondered, "keep you out of Heaven?"

"No," said Walkin' Talkin' Dave.

"Yes," said Bogie. "And I know, I'm going. Moral crimes are the only kind they keep track of. I never indulge in them."

"So," Terminal Sue said slowly, "if you kill someone, but they deserved it, is that a moral crime?"

Kathy said, "Yes."

Bogie said decisively, "No."

Kathy said indignantly, "Thou shalt not kill. It says that, in that book."

Terminal Sue let out a sigh of relief. "Good. Then I'm going." She didn't think Bogie had a good grip on many things, but this seemed to be one of them, and she was willing to take his word for it. After all, Dreadful Sam thought Bogie was going to Heaven, and Terminal Sue considered Dreadful Sam a good judge of people, even if he had sold his own soul.

Bogie lay on the other side of the wall and thought about being in Heaven with Terminal Sue. Finally, sullenly, he said, "I'm sure you're guilty of other things, though."

And you steal cars, Terminal Sue thought, but didn't say it out loud. Obviously, stealing cars wouldn't, all by itself, keep you out of Heaven.

ROCCO DENNISON SAT on the other side of the table in the interview room. He had begun the interviews with Chad the tattooed man. It had been interesting, but unproductive. Next he'd seen Doctor Death and Kathy. Together, because the jail matron had said that Kathy and Doctor Death did everything together. Rocco had sensibly insisted that the jail matron remain as he interviewed Doctor Death and Kathy. The interview had been interesting, unproductive, and arousing.

Walkin' Talkin' Dave had refused to talk to him without Blue Hair present.

Rocco spoke to Bogie for longer than he wanted to. Bogie told Rocco everything. At length. Rocco Dennison killed three roles of Tums.

"– and then this CIA agent, Neil Armstrong, he must have been seventy years old –"

Rocco interrupted. "Neil Armstrong? The astronaut?"

"Right," Bogie nodded. "This involved rocket ships."

Rocco popped a Tums into his mouth. It was nearly midnight; the Anaheim police had called the L.A.P.D., who had reached Rocco at home. Rocco had arrived in Anaheim just as the sun set. The Anaheim police had refused to allow him to interrogate anybody until they'd finished. They'd had no luck. Rocco was wishing that *he* had had no luck: Bogie Freedom seemed to regard him as a friend.

The interview concluded with some story about really good painkillers, and a pink teacup. Bogie had not seen Terminal Sue shoot anybody's clothes, he claimed. "I was whirling, Rocco. Whirling like a dervish. It was a great ride."

Rocco ate his fourth role of Tums, in one gulp, before they brought Terminal Sue in to see him.

Terminal Sue sat down at the table and stared at him.

Rocco said, "Ms. Walks-Far."

Terminal Sue waited.

Rocco sighed. "We did this before," he pointed out.

Terminal Sue grinned at him abruptly. "You lost that time, too."

"What were you and your friends doing at Disneyland today?"

Terminal Sue's grin widened. "We went to Disneyland. We were going to ride on the *It's A Small World* ride." She paused. "I was going to pick the boat we rode in."

Rocco stared at her curiously. At their earlier meeting, she hadn't seemed a smiler. "You and your friends are in an awful lot of trouble, you know that."

Terminal Sue shook her head. "Nope. I don't know that."

"That fellow Bogie," Rocco said. "He rolled over on you. He gave you all up. If I were you, I'd tell me what's going on here. You cooperate and maybe things won't go so bad for you."

"Really? And exactly what did Mr. Freedom tell you?"

Rocco hesitated.

Terminal Sue laughed at him. "Did it involve rocket ships?" Rocco colored and Terminal Sue knew that it had.

ROCCO MADE HIS way home in the cold early pre-dawn hours.

He hoped to God there was some way he could convince his superiors to just close this case. To close this case, and keep him away from all these people. And if they wouldn't, he'd been a cop for twenty-six years. He could retire.

BLUE HAIR BAILED out Bogie and Walkin' Talkin' Dave at 8:30 A.M. the following morning. She offered Terminal Sue the job of Head Bouncer, and was refused. She left the Indian woman in jail. Blue Hair bailed out her employees, and she bailed out her granddaughter. No one else.

They drove back to Los Angeles in Blue Hair's Mercedes. She made Bogie drive, made Dave sit in the front seat beside him, and sat in the back seat with her stick. "I take it," she asked, "that you have solved our Nazi problem?"

Walkin' Talkin' Dave said, "Yeah. Jeff Stone and Mitch Weber both got arrested, and nobody's going to bail *them* out. And Andrew's still around somewhere, but I don't think he's much of a threat."

"But eventually," Blue Hair said, "the other two will get out. I take it you have considered this eventuality?"

"Sure," said Bogie. "But they're not the brains of the operation. They never even tried to fight back. They just ran. And you hit Jeff Stone with your stick," he pointed out. *"He's* never going to come around again. When they get let out, they'll just get jobs and blend in. That's what I think. They'll join the Republican party and blend right into Orange County society."

In the rear view mirror, Bogie saw Blue Hair lifting the stick. He twitched and the Mercedes swerved across three lanes of freeway traffic.

Blue Hair waited until the car had steadied down, and then rapped Bogie smartly on the back of his head. "You had better be right, Mr. Freedom."

Bogie adjusted his hat. Pretending to be a chauffeur *really* sucked.

IT WAS ALMOST two P.M. when Terminal Sue's lawyer bailed her out. Terminal Sue had him bail out Doctor Death and Kathy, as well. She thought it was a morally superior act, something that might help her get into Heaven.

But then again, she'd just released them on an unsuspecting world.

Her lawyer, a bright young man who worked with one of the large downtown law firms, looked stunned when Terminal Sue fired him. "How much do I pay you, Mr. Green?"

They were walking down the steps outside the police station, heading for the parking lot. Doctor Death and Kathy trailed behind them. Sue's brother Rodrigo was waiting for her in the parking lot with her Jag, had *been* waiting since morning.

Green blinked. "Three hundred dollars an hour, Ms. Walks-Far."

"How did that old woman manage to get Bogie Freedom and Dave Bradden out of jail before you got *me* out of jail?"

The man blinked again, twice. "I'm sure I wouldn't know."

"You're fired," Terminal Sue said. She stopped and waited for Doctor Death and Kathy to catch up with her. "And you two can *walk* home." Altruism only went so far.

BOGIE PULLED UP before Dreadful Sam's house in a fine new car. He wasn't sure what kind of a car it was; it had an alarm system on it that had almost, but not quite, stopped him from borrowing it. He suspected it was one of those damn cars that had a tracer on it, and if he hadn't disabled the alarm somebody would have arrived and taken it away before he got out of the house.

He trotted up the path to the door, and lifted his hand to knock.

The door didn't open.

Bogie looked at his raised hand, then at the door. It still didn't open. He knocked – not once, not twice, but three times.

There was no answer.

Bogie stared at the door, baffled. Dreadful Sam was always home when he came to visit. He raised his hand to knock again –

The door swung open and Dreadful Sam stepped out. He was dressed as he always was, with the addition of a stained jacket. He smiled at Bogie. "Good afternoon, Bogie."

He'd left the door open and behind him, Bogie could see the house. It was empty. There was nothing in the sitting room. Nothing in the hallway beyond it, which had, only a few days ago, been lined with magical, powerful objects. "What happened to your stuff?" Bogie asked in shock.

Dreadful Sam sat down on the porch, gestured to Bogie to sit down next to him. "I've given it away," he said. "I don't need it any more."

Bogie remembered all the things in the house that he wanted, remembered Dreadful Sam calling himself Bogie's father, in the hospital that night.

Dreadful Sam glanced over at him and said dryly, "I've given you too much already."

Bogie didn't ask what. He sank down onto the porch next to Dreadful Sam. "Are you going someplace?"

"Yes." Dreadful Sam was silent for a while. "And I'm not coming back, Bogie."

It hit Bogie viciously. He felt as though Blue Hair had jabbed him in the stomach with her stick. "But, but, you *can't,*" he said with impeccable logic. "You never go anyplace . . . without me," he added.

"I'm going someplace you won't want to go," said Dreadful Sam. He paused, and smiled at Bogie with a sudden burst of pleasure. "They wouldn't have you even if you *tried* to come with me."

Bogie shut his eyes against the smart of tears. "Did you kill Claudia?"

"Yes," said Dreadful Sam gently.

"I didn't know you killed people."

"You know I'm going to Hell, Bogie. There are reasons for it. It's where I belong." Dreadful Sam said it in the same tone of voice he used when the Lakers lost, as though he were mildly annoyed, but willing to put up with it, just this once.

Bogie sat on the porch, in the sunlight, with his eyes closed. He had always thought that somehow, he would keep Dreadful Sam from going to Hell. He had thought about it sometimes, late at night. Trick the Devil. He'd read stories where people had tricked the Devil, had sold their souls and gotten away with it.

Dreadful Sam said very gently, "Those are just stories, Bogie."

"Stories come from somewhere," Bogie said in a numb voice. "*Somebody* must have done it."

"No." Dreadful Sam stood up and walked down the path to the street. He headed east down Sunset, with Bogie following him, heading inland, away from the beach. He hadn't gone walking in that direction in over thirty years. "Nobody has ever done it, and I'm not going to be the first."

The heels of Dreadful Sam's boots were run down. They made little thudding sounds against the hardtop. The boots were old, perhaps as old as Bogie Freedom. Beside him, Bogie walked almost silently, his pace matching that of the older man.

"I don't want –"

"You don't always get what you want," said Dreadful Sam. The power was fading in him; it had taken almost all he had to destroy Claudia. But if the power was gone, the senses were not. He could smell the evil that surrounded him, that called him, the evil that Bogie Freedom could walk through without being touched.

"I gave her a rose," said Dreadful Sam. "It was the first real magic I ever did. I loved her and I gave her a red rose that would last as long as our love." His eyes focused on something in the far distance. "It began to die before the month was out. Don't ever love anyone too much, Bogie. It's a mistake. It gives them a hold on you."

Bogie didn't ask who *they* were. He didn't care. There were only a few people in the world who he loved, and he didn't want to lose one of them.

Bogie walked with Dreadful Sam for a long time. Hours. They headed inland and the sun set as they walked through the city. Dreadful Sam knew when Bogie began crying, and did nothing to comfort him. The darkness closed in on them, and Dreadful Sam walked tirelessly and without stopping, with Bogie Freedom falling behind him, falling further behind him with each passing mile. Not far from Koreatown, along a desolate and dirty stretch of road, Dreadful Sam stopped and turned back to face Bogie. Bogie Freedom had stopped walking, stood exhausted, tears streaking his face, at the side of the road. Dreadful Sam took two steps back toward him. "Bogie. You better sit down."

Bogie did, all at once. He collapsed down onto the sidewalk, sat with his feet in the gutter. He slumped forward, hands sliding up over his face, knocking first his sunglasses and then his hat off, into the street at his feet. "Am I ever going to see you again?"

"You'll see me again," said Dreadful Sam. "But I won't see you."

He left Bogie Freedom sitting on the curb, crying, and turned around and walked away into another place.

WHEN HE WAS a child, they called him Sammy, except for his mother, who called him Samuel.

Samuel Highland; his father was Scots and his mother was a mix, Gypsy and Cherokee. The mix had resulted in an oddness in the boy; there were things not completely normal about Sammy. He had no friends his own age, and no enemies either, a condition that did not change much through the years, until he had neared the very end of his life, when it was far too late.

When he was as old as he would ever get, they called him Dreadful Sam, and nothing else.

He was a dead man, and he had trouble remembering things. Her face was very clear, and sometimes the sound of her voice, or the way her skin tasted when they made love. But there were many things that he did not remember; her name, or his own, or that of the boy he had left behind him, back there on the curb.

He walked, and the walking made sense, the walking was right. The road changed as he walked north, up and out of the city. He came to a single-lane road, heading north, with grass growing in a strip off to both sides of the road. The hills rose up around him, and then fell away behind once he had reached the other side. He had gone a great distance as morning approached, had left the city entirely; and the cars were rare low rumbles of sound that came blasting out of the gloom, headlights cutting aside the darkness for a short interval; and then they were gone, sound and light, and the dead man was alone again.

The spells had stopped working since her death. All of them, and it worried him as much as he allowed it to. He walked into the north, and the wind rose to meet him, icy, the wind of another time and another place. It was a senseless wind, a frozen and impersonal force that didn't care whether he was a magician or a murderer or just another man who had run out of answers, and time.

A sports car, slung low to the road, came out of nowhere and was gone almost before he was aware that it was upon him. It passed close by him, so close that the wind of its passing tugged at his long leather jacket.

He walked, and walked. It was very rhythmic, very soothing; the dead man walking in the night, fleeing the truth, pursuing redemption.

Morning turned the edge of the sky gray, off to his right; and the evil hovering around him drew close, and the next vehicle on the road was a huge eighteen-wheeler, rolling along with monstrous inertia, slamming aside the air at better than seventy miles an hour.

The evil clung to him, dragged at him. The dead man could hardly breathe through it. He plowed on through it, one determined step after another. The truck was less than a mile away, and closing, and the truck was half a mile away and he stepped into the street, and the truck was a quarter of a mile away, he walked into the oncoming headlights, and by the time the driver saw him it was far too late.

The headlights illuminated him, the light blasted back the evil so that he stood free in that last instant.

He smiled up at the horrified truck driver. The truck struck him, and his blood was red as it sprayed into the air, scarlet red, the color of roses, the color of redemption.

DREADFUL SAM'S LAST thought, as the dark angels gathered round to drag him down to Hell, was of Bogie; Bogie Freedom, who would know a greater magic than Samuel Highland had ever even aspired to.

THE WAVE FROM HELL

BOGIE, WHO HAD closed the club on Thursday, been in jail on Friday, and walked with Dreadful Sam throughout most of Saturday night, arrived at *The Rock* on Sunday morning. He expected to be fired.

He passed through the empty bar and into the back room, automatically fishing a quarter out of his pocket.

The *Space Nazis* game was gone.

It had been replaced by an ancient *Centipede* game. You didn't even play it standing up; you had to sit down to play it, in the little seats that were built into the game's frame.

Bogie slumped down into the seat in front of it, dropping his quarter onto the flat screen. A spider danced across the screen as he stared at it, eating mushrooms. He could hear voices coming from Blue Hair's office. He recognized Blue Hair's voice immediately; the other voice, a little quieter and a little less annoying, resolved itself a second later. It was Terminal Sue. He wondered what she was doing talking to Blue Hair; he wondered if Sue had decided to take the job of Head Bouncer. Bogie thought about Terminal Sue being offered the Head Bouncer's job, and wondered who Blue Hair would offer the Entertainment Director's job to. He wondered where he was going to go after Blue Hair fired him.

"Lurk," Blue Hair was saying when Bogie Freedom entered her office, "is an acceptable word." She looked at Bogie with her hateful eyes, and said, *"Woohoo* is excessive."

Terminal Sue looked vaguely relieved, and it dawned upon Bogie that she was seeking advice from Blue Hair. On a day when Bogie already felt more depressed than he'd felt since his mother's death, it was just one more thing to be depressed about. Bogie had gone to Dreadful Sam for advice; all he'd ever gotten from Blue Hair were blows and paychecks and bail money.

"If that's all, my dear," said Blue Hair, bestowing one of those hateful smiles on Terminal Sue, "Mr. Freedom and I have business."

"Did you take the bouncer job?" Bogie asked.

Terminal Sue, on her way out, shook her head. "I've got a job."

Blue Hair gestured to Bogie to seat himself in front of her desk. Bogie hated that chair; it was within reach of her stick. He thought to himself that if she hit him and *then* fired him, he was going to break her stick.

"You're a day late for work, Mr. Freedom."

"Yes," Bogie agreed.

Blue Hair nodded. "I take it you'll be on time in the future."

Behind his sunglasses, Bogie's eyes narrowed. This was some kind of incredibly subtle trick. "You're not firing me?"

"No."

"You're not hitting me?"

"No. I am trying," said Blue Hair severely, "to be nice to you in your time of grief. And you are making it very difficult."

Bogie stared at her. "I'm not grieving," he lied.

"Ms. Walks-Far is grieving," said Blue Hair. "I presume you are grieving as well. If you are *not* grieving –"

"I'm grieving some," Bogie said quickly.

"The remains of the Pedialyte are behind the bar, Mr. Freedom. I suggest that you avail yourself of it. You seem a touch pale."

Bogie felt a stirring of fear. He had never seen Blue Hair be nice before and had no idea what to make of it. "But –"

Blue Hair waved a hand at him. "You may go now," she said, and when Bogie didn't move quickly enough, tapped her stick against the top of her desk once.

Bogie fled.

Terminal Sue stood behind the bar, mixing rum, pineapple juice, and Pedialyte together. "You look pale," she said. "How's your shoulder?"

"It hurts." Bogie sat down at the bar, took the drink and sipped at it.

Terminal Sue said carefully, "Dreadful Sam left me a message." She hesitated. "I'm not sure if he knew where to get in touch with you."

"I walked with him last night. For a long time."

"He's not coming back, is he?"

"Nope."

Terminal Sue nodded slowly; it was what she had expected. "That's too bad." She stood there wiping the bartop with one of the bar rags, before realizing what she was doing. She dropped it abruptly; Blue Hair would get ideas.

The side door opened, and Andrew Peak and Walkin' Talkin' Dave came in together.

Terminal Sue's right eyebrow shot up in what Bogie thought of as her Amazing Mister Spock impression.

Of all the people in the world Terminal Sue hadn't expected to see anytime soon, Andrew Peak was right there at the top of the list.

Andrew Peak, on his part, hesitated when he saw Terminal Sue.

Walkin' Talkin' Dave laid a proud hand on Andrew's shoulder, and said, "This is our new bartender." He looked at Bogie anxiously, and added, "You have to fire someone."

Bogie shook his head. "Who? I don't have anybody I don't need."

"A bartender," Dave said. "You have to fire a bartender."

"You're the Head Bartender. *You* have to fire a bartender." Bogie shook his head again. "I'm the Entertainment Director. Bartenders aren't entertaining," he pointed out.

Andrew Peak said anxiously, "I still get the job, right?"

Bogie looked at him ungraciously. "You're a Space Nazi. I don't think —"

Terminal Sue said, "Dave was a Space Nazi too. And he works here."

"I want to write screenplays," Andrew said.

"Well," said Bogie slowly, "it's true that to be a good screenwriter, you have to start off as a waiter or bartender. Preferably," he added cunningly, *"both."*

"I'll do them both," said Andrew eagerly. "I'll do whatever you want me to do."

Bogie smiled at Walkin' Talkin' Dave. "I'll fire a bartender *and* a waiter," he told Dave. "Blue Hair's really going to love this." He recalled the day that Blue Hair had tricked him into being both the Entertainment Director and the Head Bouncer, with no increase in pay. Now he'd done it to someone else.

"Come on," said Dave to Andrew. "You gotta meet Blue Hair before you can start working here." They headed toward the back office, leaving Bogie and Terminal Sue alone again.

Walkin' Talkin' Dave reappeared a moment later, without Andrew.

"You left him alone with Blue Hair?" Bogie asked.

"Sure," said Dave. "If he survives that, he can survive anything." He paused. "What are you two doing tomorrow?"

Bogie shrugged. The club was closed on Mondays, and except for taking the Huey back in the morning he didn't have to fly tomorrow. "No plans."

"I," Terminal Sue said firmly, "am going to the beach."

Walkin' Talkin' Dave's face lit up, as if Terminal Sue had just said something wonderful. "Do you surf?"

Terminal Sue shook her head. She'd never really had time to do those recreational things. "Never learned."

"Well, tomorrow's going to be a fine day to learn. We have five foot swells until almost two in the afternoon." Dave turned to Bogie. "How about you? Is your shoulder well enough for you to go surfing?"

Bogie just looked at him. Dave wanted to rub salt water in his wound.

"It's just," said Dave, as shrieks emanated from Blue Hair's office, "that the waves are going to be really great tomorrow."

Bogie shrugged. It was his day off, he'd had a hard week, and he could wear a waterproof bandage under his wet suit. "I'm there."

TERMINAL SUE NOTICED with interest that Bogie took off his hat to surf. They had spent the day surfing, Dave getting more and more excited as the day wore on. He wouldn't tell any of them what he was excited about.

About 1:30 Dave made Bogie and Terminal Sue get out of the water. "You'll get a sunburn," Walkin' Talkin' Dave told her.

Terminal Sue didn't dignify that with a response. She was at least three shades darker than he was.

"*Please* get out of the water?" Dave asked. "You're a new surfer, and Bogie's wounded."

Terminal Sue sat on her board, with her legs in the water, watching him. "So what's going to happen?"

"Something big," said Walkin' Talkin' Dave. He could barely restrain his grin. "Something really big."

THEY WATCHED AS Walkin' Talkin' Dave paddled out into the ocean. Bogie wore his wet suit zipped all the way up to his throat, to protect the bandage that was protecting his shoulder; Terminal Sue wore a one-piece white bathing suit. They lay on their blanket watching Walkin' Talkin' Dave get smaller and smaller.

"What do you think he's up to?" Terminal Sue asked.

Bogie, a longtime surfer, said flatly, "He's catching a wave." He was suffused with envy; it was going to be a *good* wave.

Terminal Sue said doubtfully, "He's going awfully far out."

"It's going to be a really big wave," Bogie said. Even as he spoke, the first glowing fragments came streaking across the sky, visible even in the mid-day sun.

Terminal Sue stared up at it, along with the rest of the crowd on Santa Monica beach. "What the hell is –" She shut up abruptly.

She knew what it was.

THE WATER CARESSED his skin, warm and friendly. He could hear the people on the shore, calling out to each other as the meteoric fragments fell overhead, but the voices were faint and far away, and getting fainter with each passing moment.

The main body of the ship was going to come down just about a mile off shore.

He pushed into it, swimming hard. He'd figured he needed to be a good half mile away from the point of impact if he was going to catch this one; it was going to rise early, and run a great long distance before beginning to peak.

THE WAVE SWEPT in toward the shore. Enormous, reaching up toward the sun, three or four times larger than the biggest wave Bogie had ever seen. Walkin' Talkin' Dave Bradden was a small speck in the midst of the water, three quarters of the way up the side of the huge wall.

The sound came from a great distance, but there was no mistaking it.

"Woohoo!"

Bogie Freedom said complacently, "*Woohoo* is too an acceptable word."

Epilogue

ON TUESDAY MORNING, April Morrissey called the number listed in the phone book. That bastard Mike thought he could get away with cheating on her, but she'd show him.

An answering machine picked up. "You've reached the offices of the Walks-Far Detective Agency. We're closed right now. We're going to remain closed for a good while. The owner has gone to the beach to practice her surfing and isn't coming back until she's damn good and ready."

The answering machine clicked off without giving April a chance to leave a message. April stared at the phone for a second. *"Fine,"* she said furiously. She started looking through her junk drawer. That guy, the one who wore the hat, the one over at the club. He did investigations. Successful investigations. She'd heard.

She came up with the business card. Bogie Freedom. She eyed the card doubtfully; it didn't say private investigator. It said *Entertainment Director, The Rock*. She shrugged, and began dialing. Maybe it was a cover.

Tom Rochester *swore* the guy was the best.

www.ingramcontent.com/pod-product-compliance
Lightning Source LLC
Chambersburg PA
CBHW070547160426

43199CB00014B/2405